941.1B · 173   ①
370 reet

Antitrust
Policies
and
Issues

PERSPECTIVES ON ECONOMICS SERIES

Michael L. Wachter & Susan M. Wachter, Editors

PUBLISHED

**Development, The International Economic Order
and Commodity Agreements,** *Jere R. Behrman*
Labor Unions, *George H. Hildebrand*
Economics of Health, *Joseph Newhouse*
Monetarism, *William Poole*
Antitrust Policies and Issues, *Roger Sherman*
Income Distribution and Redistribution, *Paul J. Taubman*

AVAILABLE LATE 1978 AND EARLY 1979

Labor Unions, *George H. Hildebrand*
Forecasting *Lawrence R. Klein & Michael M. Young*
International Trade, *Stephen P. Magee*
Regulation, *Roger G. Noll*
Population, *T. Paul Schultz*
Urban Economics, *Michael L. Wachter*

Antitrust Policies and Issues

Roger Sherman

University of Virginia

▲
▼▼
ADDISON-WESLEY PUBLISHING COMPANY
Reading, Massachusetts • Menlo Park, California
London • Amsterdam • Don Mills, Ontario • Sydney

This book is in the
ADDISON-WESLEY SERIES IN ECONOMICS

Michael and Susan Wachter
Consulting Editors

ISBN 0-201-08363-9
ABCDEFGHIJK-AL-798

Foreword

The PERSPECTIVES ON ECONOMICS series has been developed to present economics students with up-to-date policy-oriented books written by leading scholars in this field. Many professors and students have stressed the need for flexible, contemporary materials that provide an understanding of current policy issues.

In general, beginning students in economics are not exposed to the controversial material and development of current issues that are the basis of research in economics. Because of their length and breadth of coverage, textbooks tend to lack current economic thinking on policy questions; in attempting to provide a balanced viewpoint, they often do not give the reader a feel for the lively controversy in each field. With this series, we have attempted to fill this void.

The books in this series are designed to complement standard textbooks. Each volume reflects the research interests and views of the authors. Thus these books can also serve as basic reading material in the specific topic courses covered by each. The stress throughout is on the careful development of institutional factors and policy in the context of economic theory. Yet the exposition is designed to be accessible to undergraduate students and interested laypersons with an elementary background in economics.

Michael L. Wachter
Susan M. Wachter

Preface

Antitrust policy is supposed to prevent monopoly, restraint of trade, or other unfair practices in our economy. Although partly successful in these aims, it has not been applied very consistently since it came into being with the Sherman Act in 1890. That act was vaguely worded and remains so today, even though the businessmen who are subject to it and the jurists who must enforce it both would prefer more precise statutes. Yet, politicians seem unable to agree on the more precise goals that might be held out for antitrust policy. And even where they could agree, they might accept a vague law rather than offend powerful elements in their constituencies by taking definitive positions, with the result that details of antitrust policy pass to bureaucrats and federal judges who do not have to face reelection. Without more precise legislative guidance for the courts, the conflicting rights of parties often can prevent decisive antitrust action. More knowledge of the antitrust problem may enable us to find a better solution than we have. It is with that hope, at least, that antitrust aims, history, enforcement, ultimate effects, and proposals for reform are portrayed here.

In the summer of 1976 I visited the University College at Buckingham, England, and am grateful that I could take advantage of its fine law library and congenial environment to work on this book. Since then many persons have added to the pleasure of the work. Specific suggestions by Richard Schramm, James Sell, and Ingo Vogelsang were very helpful. Phillip Grossman provided research assistance. For invaluable comments on earlier versions of the entire manuscript I thank especially Kenneth Elzinga, Larry Fullerton, John James, Michael Wachter, and Judge Seymour Wenner. My greatest debt is to Michael Moohr, whose help and encouragement, so fundamental it has to be called teaching, added much to the historical treatment of the subject. The book is dedicated to those who read it, with the hope that they will demand more from antitrust policy in the years to come.

R. S.

Charlottesville, Virginia
March 1978

Contents

Introduction 1

Near the end of the nineteenth century a fresh and unified approach to design called Art Nouveau arose and flourished. It used asymmetrical flaming shapes with a distinctive bravado and inventiveness. Although rooted in the Gothic tradition, with its asymmetry, organic shapes, and bright colors, Art Nouveau appeared as a sudden break from what went before it, those mass-produced and standardized products of the industrial revolution. And while the Art Nouveau style lasted little more than a decade, it opened the way for what we think of as modern design.

At about the same time in the United States there was a response to another unwanted by-product of the industrial revolution, market control by combinations of corporations using unfair business practices. The response took the form of the Sherman Act, which was worded like a constitutional amendment summarily branding as illegal all monopolizing and restraint of trade. It too had roots in the past, in common law, but it was a new and necessarily experimental form of legislation to deal with a growing economic problem. As it became effective and was joined with further antitrust legislation, the Sherman Act also appeared to be a sharp break from the past, a change almost as striking as Art Nouveau had been in the world of design. But antitrust legislation never passed to a new stage for the modern world. Today it remains an institution built of turn-of-the-century ideas, leaving major questions of economic policy persistently unresolved.

This is not to say that the Sherman Act with its consequent antitrust policy has had no effect. Whether you attend a movie or buy a box of cornflakes, you can be affected by antitrust policy. Although not as visual as a new design, the effects are still there: perhaps in the price you have to pay, in the parties that may serve you and the convenience of their locations, or maybe in determining whether you may buy one item without having to purchase another one with it as well. It is not surprising that antitrust policy actions remain largely invisible to most of us, because the goal of antitrust policy is not really to *control* economic activity anyway. Rather it attempts to preserve and promote competition, the accepted means of controlling economic activity in the United States today.

Antitrust policy, its shape, accomplishments, weaknesses, and avenues for improvement, is the subject of this book. In this chapter the ground is prepared for a study of antitrust policy by examining business enterprise, the market process and the functioning of law and politics. We turn more fully to a consideration of the economic aims of antitrust policy in Chapter 2. The actual development of our antitrust laws is traced in Chapter 3, and their enforcement is examined in Chapter 4. After an attempt to gauge the effects of past antitrust policies on the U.S. enomomy in Chapter 5, alternative laws and policies that are urged for achieving the same or other goals will be discussed in Chapter 6.

TRUSTS AND CORPORATIONS

The terms *trust* and *antitrust* date from the nineteenth century. The "voting trust" first came into use in 1882 when the shareholders of fifty oil refineries surrendered their stock for certificates in the Standard Oil Trust [4, pp. 518-19]. Although trusts were found unlawful in some states, many of them, including the Standard Oil Trust, persisted undeterred until the federal antitrust Sherman Act was passed in 1890. Another trust-like device used at the close of the nineteenth century was the *holding company,* in which a majority of the voting stock of concerns to be combined would be gathered together. The concerns looked independent but since all their directors were elected by the holding company their policies could be coordinated. That same result also could be achieved by *interlocking director- ates,* which resulted when the same persons were directors of several impor- tant firms in a single industry.

Not surprisingly, in popular use the word "trust" came to mean mono- poly. Of course large business enterprise and monopoly are not the same thing, for monopoly power to set price and deny entry to a market does not require, or necessarily accompany, large-scale business enterprise. A market that is small might be monopolized by a small firm, whereas many large corporations might compete vigorously in a large market. But the trusts controlled large parts of their markets, and in the early years of this century we went through what is called the "trust-busting" era under presidents Theodore Roosevelt, William Howard Taft and Woodrow Wilson, limiting the use of outright trusts mainly to public service companies like railroads and public utilities overseen by state or other regulatory authorities. It is interesting to observe how forms of business organization developed, passing through this trust form and leading to what we see today as the modern corporation.

At the end of the seventeenth century, when it was first employed in Europe as a so-called joint stock company, the shareholder form of business organization was drastically misused. A number of joint stock companies formed in England and France later collapsed as their organizers ran off with the funds or proved incompetent. One of the most famous was the South Sea Company, which assumed England's national debt in 1711 in return for an annual payment of interest plus a monopoly over British trade with the South Sea Islands and South America. Speculation drove the price of shares in the company far out of proportion to their value and fraud was exposed in the collapse that followed. The event came to be known as the South Sea Bubble and it led in 1720 to what was called the Bubble Act in England, a law that effectively prevented widespread use of this organizational form for a hundred years. Because of such a history, any organization resembling a corporation was regarded with suspicion in the United States during the early colonial period.

In eighteenth century America the archetypal corporation actually was a municipality. We were well into the nineteenth century before the corporation came into use in private business [10]. New York first allowed a business firm to incorporate itself in 1811; the corporation then could have capital of only $100,000 and a life of only twenty years [15]. The significance of the New York law was in allowing voluntary incorporation as a routine bureaucratic procedure under specific terms, rather than by special act of a state legislature open only to businessmen with political influence (sometimes through corruption) [18]. By midcentury railroads predominated among corporations. Manufacturing corporations became numerous after the Civil War, and by 1900 much of our commerce and industry was conducted by corporations.

Governmental power to create corporations was retained by the individual states, and in granting charters through most of the 1800s the states imposed harsh requirements. A corporation typically had to serve a well-defined purpose such as providing railroad transportation between two specific points; as in New York it had a limited life and could accumulate only a specified amount of capital. The corporation also was forbidden from owning stock in another corporation. But states abandoned many of these restrictions when they began to compete with each other to raise revenue by granting corporate charters in the 1890s. In particular, New Jersey allowed one corporation to own another, thereby giving corporation status to holding companies and trusts. Among its customers was the Standard Oil Company that was created from portions of the Standard Oil Trust. The modern business corporation with its wide range of rights and powers was born during this period.

The present-day corporation is a legal invention allowing shareholders a sophisticated property interest in a business enterprise. This ownership interest can be quite separate from the actual *operation* of the business, as any holder of a few shares in a large corporation well knows, because shareholders of a corporation may elect a board of directors to oversee the salaried top managers of the business. Liability is limited to the amount of money the shareholder has invested so there is no worry about being dragged into court to settle further obligations of the enterprise. However, shareholding owners retain a residual claim to the net assets and net income of the corporation. Like a person the corporation may sue and be sued and it also pays taxes, but as long as it is solvent it does not die; it has perpetual life. By contrast, the proprietorship and partnership forms of business enterprise end abruptly when the owner or a partner dies. And a proprietor, or any partner, also may be held liable for obligations beyond the investments they have made in the business. With this burden of potential liability it is not surprising that proprietors and partners take a careful and active part in managing the businesses they own.

Table 1.1 Importance of major forms of business organizations, 1973

Form of organization	Manufacturing only			All sectors of economy		
	Number (thousands)	Sales (billions)	Net profit (billions)	Number (thousands)	Sales (billions)	Net profit (billions)
Corporation	209	$1,002	$63	1,905	$2,558	$120
Partnership	30	7	1	1,039	124	9
Proprietorship	210	9	1	10,648	311	47

Source: Statistical Abstract of the United States (Washington, D.C.: Bureau of the Census, 1976), p. 507.

More commercial activity is carried out by corporations in the United States today than by businesses under all other forms of organization. Table 1.1 reveals this importance of corporations for the year 1973. In that year 85 percent of all sales were handled by corporations; corporations actually could claim 98 percent of reported sales in manufacturing alone. And because some corporations also control unincorporated dealers or franchise operators, the total control probably is greater than even these figures suggest. Of course corporations operate under more restrictive conditions now than in the South Sea Bubble days. In the United States they are regulated by many governmental bodies and are subject to detailed reporting and disclosure rules by the Securities and Exchange Commission (SEC) in order to protect investors. Nevertheless there is concern that hired managers may not operate these organizations entirely in the interests of their owners; where they do, competition may not force them to serve the general consuming public well. For there also is concern about the degree of monopoly in the economy and the fairness of competition that exists today.

Corporate power and industrial monopoly are modern problems. The industrial revolution ushered in our modern age with its large organizations and greatly expanded use of capital overseen by a whole new capitalist class that controls production by time clocks, production lines, and scientific management. Such new methods brought with them disputes that old rules which had served for centuries were inadequate to resolve, and a new set of rules was needed. Antitrust law in the United States represents a unique effort to have the legal process enforce competition in the marketplace and, in that way, to guide business practice.

But let us not get ahead of our story. Since we shall be concerned with the private enterprise market process that we rely on in the United States, we shall first discuss it briefly. Then we shall discuss the legal process that affects the working of that market process and remark about the political process that produced our antitrust laws. We shall then be in position to examine antitrust in the remaining chapters.

MARKETS

For more than a thousand years, from about A.D.500 to A.D.1500, feudal manorial organization guided economic activity throughout western Europe, where workers without very specialized training tilled soil and tended animals in predominantly agrarian societies. Typically, land was not individually owned in the modern sense of being readily saleable, and economic activities were sustained mainly by tradition. Goods were made largely for local consumption instead of being bought, transported, and sold as they commonly are today. During this period, before military weapons such as gunpowder or even the cross-bow were developed, the important political entities were small kingdoms, which could be defended easily, rather than the great nations of today.[1]

If we could watch the sort of trading that occurred in market towns late in this medieval period (imagine parties haggling amid piles of produce without the aid of currency, let alone credit cards) we might think it primitive and chaotic. But behind the scenes it was closely controlled. As early as the eleventh century, guild organizations were given royal charters to regulate trade in English towns. And great trading companies like the famous East India Company (and the infamous South Sea Company) held royal charters to oversee foreign trade; by the fifteenth century they exercised power in foreign countries much as an arm of government would.

At that time the granting by kings of exclusive royal charters to particular groups seemed a sensible way to control economic activity; it also did not appear to have the restrictive effects of monopoly. But at the end of the sixteenth century, under Queen Elizabeth, these grants began to be made to individuals, sometimes as patents for new inventions (often to foreigners so their technology could be attracted to England), and they took on more obvious monopolistic advantages. Some grants were virtually sold just to raise revenue for the Crown; others went as rewards to loyal friends.

After abuse of monopoly grants by the Crown became apparent, Parliament, the political body that had grown from small advisory councils of local leaders in the medieval period, sought to restrain it. Parliament found an avenue for this in the arguments of Sir Edward Coke, chief justice under King James I, who insisted that the common law (and not the king) was the supreme law of the land. While some decisions at common law courts were helping competitive trade the merchants and traders who were well represented in Parliament passed laws that changed property rights to foster even more commercial activity.

As an example of the changes that occurred by legislative act we might single out enclosures, the fencing of fields for individual rather than cooperative use of common land. Common use of land by many parties had developed when land had been plentiful. But in the sixteenth century, when land was scarce and the price of wool was high, exclusive rights to land actually could raise wool production by preventing the overgrazing that was resulting on common land.[2] Parliament passed a series of Enclosure Acts that narrowed the common uses for land and permitted the formation, by sale and purchase of land, of large estates.[3] Enclosures also allowed efficient land use as crops became relatively more valuable in the seventeenth century. When new livestock feeds, such as clover, were introduced from America and the turnip was brought from Holland, changes in the sizes and shapes of plots became appropriate and exclusive property rights fostered their formation [12]. The Enclosure Acts alone did not cause the industrial revolution; they affected only a fraction of all land and the industrial revolution visited some countries that never undertook the enclosure of land that was adopted in England [6]. But the enclosures typify the move toward more exact property rights facilitating trade.

The trade and commerce that developed in England, especially after the Revolutionary War and independence for America, was spectacular. Macadam roads were built, canals were dug, and in the 1800s railroads stretched from city to city. A system of banks developed and facilitated the raising of capital. Between 1780 and 1860 more political restraints on trade were removed. For instance, laws from the 1400s had regulated the supplies of small grains to keep their prices high. After much debate, these laws, called the Corn Laws, were repealed in 1846. New technological discoveries were made and modern science found profitable application. Where life had stood almost in the same place for many centuries, in the eighteenth and nineteenth centuries the modern world began to emerge.

Of this burst of economic activity Arnold Toynbee observed "[t]he essence of the Industrial Revolution is the substitution of competition for the medieval regulations which had previously controlled the production and distribution of wealth."[4] The working of this competitive market process was described masterfully by Adam Smith [19], who saw clearly how actions by individual agents, all seeking their own best interests, could serve society well if all agents were subject to the pressures of competitive markets. Of course any one seller might seek to profit very much on a transaction; but if customers could go elsewhere that seller would be constrained by competitors' prices. As a result, market prices would tend to approximate the full costs of goods that were efficiently produced, with nothing left over as wastefully excessive profit.

In the right circumstances effective competition can bring prices roughly into line with costs of production. In addition, market prices actually can guide production. For example, suppose a good's competitive market price were well above the long-run cost of production. This would mean that consumers valued that good at more than it would cost to produce it on a long-run basis. So there would be high profit that would spur expansion by existing producers and invite entry by new producers. A system of competitive markets would move resources—capital, workers, managers, materials—to increase the production of these goods that consumers valued so much. The expanded quantities would make the goods more plentiful and force market price down until it was again close to the cost of production so further expansion of output no longer was motivated.

When monopoly is present this market process is not as effective because the price of a good or service may lie above long-run cost without bringing expanded production. A monopoly limits the supply of the good or service and thereby keeps its price high. Consumers could be benefited by more production of the good since they value it highly; after all, to buy from a monopoly they must place a higher value on the last units produced than those units actually cost. Modern antitrust policy has tried to prevent these unwanted consequences of monopoly and see to it that competition functions in its place. The instrument most relied upon in this effort is the process of the law.

LAW

Many legal concepts are relevant to economic affairs. The notion of a contract, for example, is important in law and is basic to economic transactions. We have just seen how the exclusive ownership right fostered efficient resource allocation in the example of the Enclosures Acts, which encouraged efficient land use in England because they allowed land to be exchanged rather than merely held by tradition in return for services rendered. Of course we all take for granted a great range of ownership rights today. One ticket gives you the right to sit in a particular theater seat for a specified evening, while another lets you reclaim your hat after the performance. Private property involves a vast number of legal claims that can apply even when ownership is separated from possession, with many duties and liabilities as well as ownership advantages all upheld by law.[5]

Through the ages, all civilizations have had to form some system of law in order to organize governments and settle disputes; the Western nations that rely heavily on markets to guide economic activities are not exceptions. Of course what law *is* changes with time, just as laws themselves change. Influenced by science and empirical methods of the nineteenth century, John Austin [1] first set out a positive notion of law, focusing on law not as it ought to be but as it really is. Up to that time a pure theory of law had been claimed to exist quite independent of other bodies of knowledge, as a set of norms based largely on the inherent nature of man and God. At the turn of the century, after achievements in biology by Charles Darwin and Herbert Spencer and in legal history by Sir Henry Maine [13], anthropological and historical views of law appeared, searching for broad principles as a basis for law. Maine claimed, for example, that for settling disputes the gradual shift from authority or *status* to *contract* under law was a good development for social relations. By that time contrasting views by Karl Marx [14], which challenged the indispensability of law, became more widely known. Marx found defects and inequalities in society were due not to the nature of man but to the way his economic affairs were organized. Law was seen by Marx as an instrument of domination that could decline in influence just as the state itself eventually could decline.

A great many sociological theories of law have been advanced in the last two hundred years, also. These theories were often normative in that they sought scientific principles that could guide the improvement of society. But they were objective enough to try to see how law works. Jeremy Bentham [2; 3] saw laws as balancing the collectivist interests of society against the private interests. More purposefully, Roscoe Pound [17] viewed law as a way of taking social facts into account to engineer an efficient social structure, thereby to balance efficiently individual interests, public interests, and social interests. A modern realism school currently uses social science to examine the legal process. They accept law generally as "what the judges decide," and try to improve it by predicting more fully the ultimate effects of legal decisions using knowledge from the social sciences.

In describing this process of the law in more detail it is useful to distinguish *criminal* law from *civil* law. Criminal law is a set of rules we all must obey or face punishment by the state. Governments force adherence to these rules of criminal law, which may vary from place to place but usually include arson, bigamy, forgery, murder, and treason, because the rules are judged to be needed for society's survival. Civil law, on the other hand, includes rules for business affairs, the transfer of property, and the recovery of money for injuries through the fault of others. Civil and criminal law are not mutually exclusive, for many offenses may be both civil and criminal. *Torts* are civil wrongs for which an injured party may recover damages because the injury was deliberate or due to carelessness; slander, trespassing, or car theft are all interpreted as violations of an individual's rights and are torts. In most jurisdictions the theft of a car, like the theft of a horse many years ago, would also be considered a crime.

Two main systems of law used by Western nations are Roman law and English law. Roman law derives from the earliest forms of law. It relies on deliberate lawmaking by legislative and judicial bodies to produce clear rules for regulating human affairs; most western European countries use it. To decide cases under Roman law, courts look to the text of the statutes or legal codes set out by higher authority, whereas under English law they look more to past court decisions. While English law gives greater scope to judges in interpreting the law on a case-by-case basis, it is also the hallmark of the English common law system that judicial *precedent* is binding on judges [4, p. 28] through a common law doctrine which is given the Latin name of *stare decisis*. *Stare decisis* applies not to the particular decision in a dispute[6] but rather to the rule of law that is involved in reaching the decision and requires that it be adhered to in the future. Obviously, collecting rules of law this way was possible only after reliable reports of previous cases became available. A settled hierarchy of courts also helped to determine which rules would be binding, for *stare decisis* was brought into operation by reference to the decisions of higher courts.

The United States follows English law rather than Roman law, with slight exceptions. (Under French influence, the state of Louisiana adopted much Roman law, and California and Texas retain traces of Spanish law, which is of the Roman type.) In England the rule of English law depends on criteria established by acts of parliament, by the principles followed in previous judicial decisions (which would be called judicial precedent), or by immemorial custom. England has no constitution to serve as a source of law, but if no primary law or principle is available to help in deciding a case, a court may turn to foreign law, legal textbooks, or even social values as sources of law. Criteria are similar here in the United States, with acts of Congress, judicial precedent, and custom being major sources of law, although we also have the United States Constitution (as amended) as a continual source of law.

Legislation of some kind is widely regarded as "indispensible to the efficient regulation of the modern state" [7, p. 77]. And as long as they do not conflict with the Constitution, legislative statutes take priority over judicial opinion. In the United States the judicial branch has responsibility for interpreting the Constitution; federal courts can find an act of legislation to be in conflict with the Constitution and overturn it. Or an act of legislation may be worded vaguely and judges must interpret its statutes, trying to plumb the purpose of the legislation so they can render a judgment accordingly. Legislation itself results from a political process that obviously has an important role in shaping antitrust policy.

POLITICS

Where, if anywhere, should power to control economic affairs be lodged? We have seen that the right to own, use, or exchange property has developed over many hundreds of years to the point where all sorts of goods and services are exchanged reliably in markets by means of subtle forms of the property right, from theater tickets to shares in the ownership of business firms. If distributed somewhat evenly among us, these rights to property can disperse economic power into many hands and thereby support democratic government, with little need for centralized power. But, if unevenly distributed, economic power can cause political power to be unevenly distributed also, making the rich—even when their riches are owed to monopoly advantage—hard to control.

Well-defined property rights actually have prevented state government from interfering with the affairs of its citizens, whether for antitrust or for a different goal. On several occasions in the nineteenth century the Supreme Court found actions of individual states unconstitutional for violating contracts previously entered into.[7] That limitation seriously constrained state action against monopoly power. The right of a state to regulate the price of a public service was finally established in the famous *Munn* v. *Illinois*[8] decision, which paved the way for establishing state regulatory commissions to oversee public utilities. But remember that the Fourteenth Amendment was added to the Constitution after the Civil War and it required that "no person shall be deprived of life, liberty, or property without due process of law." When the Supreme Court accepted the private corporation as a *person* in 1886, it thereby extended to corporations the protection of the Fourteenth Amendment which meant that corporations were entitled to due process as persons. As a result, states could not penalize corporations arbitrarily under state antitrust laws [16, pp. 41-49]. Much debate about the Sherman Act focused on whether it would conflict with the Fifth Amendment, which requires the federal government to follow due process procedures as well.[9]

Thus government action, such as is involved in antitrust policy, may encounter principles of equity that can stand in the way of improving the functioning of our market process. The question those nineteenth century cases faced might go something like this. If a business firm has behaved according to the rules of the game implicit in current laws and previous court decisions, making sizeable investments on the presumption those rules will continue in force, is it reasonable to change them, say by passing a radically new law or reaching a new and unexpected court decision? Actions that change property rights and rules of the game may benefit some and harm others. Not only may they be unfair, but arbitrary changes may lead parties to worry about possible future changes and not plan as efficiently as a result. Some changes are necessary, of course, but stability and continuity are also desirable. Actions must be taken carefully so they can develop consistently and not upset and frustrate sound planning. Yet if we follow that line of reasoning too far, powerful economic interests may persist indefinitely in unfair and inefficient performance.

What we are noting here is that perfect governmental or legal remedies are not available for many of the situations an antitrust policy faces. Advantages currently enjoyed by some producers may be so long established that changing them now will be difficult. Those who are benefiting financially from their current positions can hire excellent counsel, present their case persuasively to legislators and government administrators, and perhaps as a result keep the rules working in their favor. Not only does government lack unlimited power to alter contract, property, and other legal relations in our society, it also is influenced by those very persons it is called upon to control. Also, throughout American history many have believed small business units to be the backbone of an ideal Jeffersonian democracy, and have wanted to foster rugged individualism of the sort possessed by frontier farmers. But those same aims might be claimed by increasingly powerful businessmen, who could associate individualism with laissez-faire policy that would prevent government interference with established economic power.

The making of laws lies in the hands of those who control the legislative machinery, and to a lesser extent the judicial machinery, of government. They are not just a small group so it is not surprising that laws usually reflect the status quo, tending to continue the existing order but accommodating peacefully and orderly to change. Although behavior in keeping with our laws has long been cloaked in respectability and legitimacy, from time to time laws on the books have been challenged. They have been labeled "wrong" and significant numbers of citizens have refused to obey them. Close observation of the political process and of recent cases of civil disobedience shows that laws can indeed be wrong; they are authored by politically dominant groups who can insinuate their own preferences into law, and the results do not always deserve the authority usually reserved for law. We point out this potential fallibility in law, and in law making, not so much to criticize the process as to remind readers that the process is imperfect, and that a study of it should take this possibility into account.

SUMMARY

The industrial revolution is behind us. As a society we can no more reject large organizations to pursue only family and parochial production concerns, or do without capital and scientific method and return to a predominantly rural life, than we as individuals can forget all we have learned since the first grade in school. But neither can we claim that the spectacular transition of the last two hundred years, from agrarian communities to modern industrial nations, has gone perfectly. Modern life seems to require ever more elaborate political and economic organizations. At least we are finding again and again that our organizations are inadequate to meet our needs. So we approach this examination of antitrust policy in a critical way, with the hope that readers can find improvements that may very well be needed in the near future.

So far we have described the now dominant commercial organization, the corporation, and considered generally the economic, legal and political processes functioning in the United States. We now turn to consider more carefully the advantages of competition that antitrust laws, primarily the Sherman Act, the Clayton Act, and the Federal Trade Commission Act, presumably are intended to achieve. In successive chapters we shall then see the laws and how they were enacted, how they have been enforced, what their consequences are today, and some major alternative laws that might be considered in their place.

REFERENCES

1. John Austin. *Lectures on Jurisprudence, or the Philosophy of Positive Law.* Robert Campbell, ed. New York: J. Cockcroft and Co., 1875.

2. Jeremy Bentham. *An Introduction to the Principles of Morals and Legislation.* Oxford: The Clarendon Press, 1879.

3. Jeremy Bentham. *The Limits of Jurisprudence Defined* (written in 1782 and first printed from the author's manuscript with an introduction by Charles Warren Everett). New York: Columbia University Press, 1945.

4. Victor S. Clark. *History of Manufactures in the United States, 1860-1914.* Washington, D. C.: Carnegie Institution, 1928.

5. Ronald H. Coase. "The Problem of Social Cost." *Journal of Law and Economics,* 3:1-44 (October 1960).

6. Phyllis Deane. *The First Industrial Revolution.* Cambridge: Cambridge University Press, 1965.

7. R. W. M. Dias. *Jurisprudence.* London: Butterworth and Co., Ltd., 1964.

8. J. E. Christopher Hill. *The Century of Revolution.* Edinburgh: Thomas Nelson and Sons, Ltd., 1961.

9. Michael Howard. *War in European History*. London: Oxford University Press, 1976.

10. Morton J. Horwitz. *The Transformation of American Law*. Cambridge, Mass.: Harvard University Press, 1977.

11. D. Lasok and J. W. Bridge, *An Introduction to the Law and Institutions of the European Communities*. London: Butterworth and Co., Ltd., 1973.

12. Douglass C. North and Robert Paul Thomas. *The Rise of the Western World*. Cambridge: Cambridge University Press, 1973.

13. Henry S. Maine. *Ancient Law*. London: John Murray, 1920.

14. Karl H. Marx. *Capital*. Trans. by Eden and Cedar Paul. London: George Allen and Unwin, Ltd., 1928 (1867).

15. Edward S. Mason. "Corporation," in *International Encyclopedia of the Social Sciences*, Vol. 3. New York: Crowell Collier and Macmillan, 1968.

16. Arthur Selwyn Miller. *The Modern Corporate State*. Westport, Conn.: Greenwood Press, 1976.

17. Roscoe Pound. *Jurisprudence*, Vols. I-V. St. Paul, Minn.: West Publishing Co., 1959.

18. Henry R. Seager and Charles A. Gulick, Jr. *Trust and Corporation Problems*. New York: Harper and Brothers, 1929.

19. Adam Smith. *The Wealth of Nations*. New York: The Modern Library, 1937 (1776).

20. Arnold Toynbee, *Toynbee's Industrial Revolution*, New York: Augustus M. Kelley, 1969 (1884).

END NOTES

1. There were economic as well as military advantages in the small kingdoms. See [9].

2. Enclosure of pastoral land had precedent in common law as early as 1236 in the Statute of Merton. See [12, p. 150].

3. See [8]. That the Enclosure Acts helped the rich inherit the earth is felicitously expressed in this poem [8, p. 151]:

   The law locks up the man or woman
   That steals the goose from off the common;
   But leaves the greater villain loose
   Who steals the common from the goose.

4. See [20, p. 85]. I am grateful to Max Hartwell for pointing out this Toynbee passage.

5. Professor Ronald Coase provides an excellent analysis of the crucial role property rights play in the functioning of markets [5].

6. After the time for appealing a court decision has passed, that decision is binding on the parties involved and cannot be disputed in any subsequent proceeding between them, according to a legal principle called *res judicata*.

7. See *Fletcher* v. *Peck*, 10 U. S. 87 (1810), and *Trustees of Dartmouth College* v. *Woodward*, 17 U. S. 518 (1819). Both of these opinions were written by John Marshall.

8. *Munn* v. *Illinois*, 94 U. S. 113 (1877).

9. Ways for government to influence economic processes are quite different among Western countries. For discussion see [11].

Economic Aims For **2**
Antitrust

When price rises above cost in a competitive market, producers expand and new firms enter, with the result that price is driven back down toward the level of cost. As a result prices in competition reflect costs faithfully. Then in choosing among goods and services by comparing prices consumers will actually be comparing true relative costs. Under monopoly organization of a market, on the other hand, the pressure to minimize costs can almost vanish. And the monopoly price will tend to be above the resulting high cost. With some monopoly prices and some competitive prices from which to choose, consumers looking at all prices will no longer be able to see the relative costs of alternative goods and services; therefore, they will be misled about the true economic opportunities that relative costs represent. There are also other complaints one reasonably can make about monopoly.

Still it is not enough to say that antitrust laws are "to make of ours . . . a competitive business economy,"[1] because competition will not always function well. There are technological circumstances, like economies of large scale, that handicap competition. And there are benefits from technical progress that the prize of patent monopoly can encourage. In view of these real-world conditions our antitrust policy has necessarily been flexible; instead of precisely defined rules we have a general policy aim of relying on competition and denying monopoly, depending on the possibilities available. Courts have fashioned practical guidelines from specific cases in an effort to achieve these general aims.

Here we shall look at the advantages of competition for controlling economic activity and also examine the principal problems a monopoly causes. Rather than stop with the one-sided analysis we should have at that point, showing competition preferable to monopoly, we must go on to describe circumstances encountered in the world that prevent our relying solely on the process of market competition. Then finally we can discuss general aims for antitrust policy and even note some ways to assess their achievement.

WHY FAVOR COMPETITION?

Although it may seem strange to describe a system of competitive markets as a communication and information system, that is really a useful way to view it. A competitive market system enables consumers to tell suppliers just what to produce. Furthermore, their instructions to suppliers can be based on knowledge of the true costs of alternative goods and services, knowledge provided to them through market prices. As an institution for informing consumers and relaying their instructions to producers, the market system is really quite remarkable. When its prices provide the right signals it manifests a high level of efficiency, and yet it can also be equitable. We must be careful to define efficiency clearly, though, so we can evaluate the effectiveness of prices for achieving it.

One view of efficiency is widely understood. It is the concept of getting the largest possible output from any given collection of inputs, or minimizing the cost of producing whatever quantity is produced of any good or service. Having many competing producers, and still more who will become producers as the price rises, will ordinarily make low-cost production an essential goal for any one producer in order to survive. The presence of many competing producers plus free entry to an industry will enforce this cost-minimizing efficiency.

There is another concept of efficiency that may be less familiar, particularly to noneconomists, but is no less important. This second concept of efficiency focuses on the process of choosing how much of which goods and services should be produced. It is important because there can be little benefit from producing goods that consumers do not want, even at minimum cost. A market system especially excels in this second interpretation of efficiency. Of course both notions of efficiency must be present if an economy is to be truly efficient overall, having the best mixture of output quantities as well as lowest cost production.

The real key to achieving economic efficiency is having the price of a product equal the value of all the resources—labor, material, capital equipment—that are absolutely needed to make one of the last, often called marginal, units of that product.[2] When prices of products are equal to their marginal unit costs, all consumers, in making their purchase decisions, will face prices that reflect precisely the current technical opportunities open to them. After comparing prices, a person's choice of a polo shirt rather than a sweater is based not only on the person's taste but also on how easy it is for society to turn out a polo shirt or a sweater, which is reflected in the price of a polo shirt relative to that of a sweater.

It is freedom of entry into any activity that lets market prices send resources where they satisfy our preferences as consumers best while at the same time bringing pressure for cost-minimizing production. As we noted in Chapter 1, a price above marginal cost indicates a profit opportunity that, under competition, will attract more resources to the production of the product. Each firm that newly enters the market may have a small effect on price, but as more and more firms enter and more units are produced, market price will tend to fall; the last unit produced will be valued less and less by consumers until finally the price will equal marginal cost. No extra high profit will remain as incentive to enter the industry then and average cost will be as low as possible because high-cost producers will lose money and be unable to survive.

These efficiency ideas and the essence of the market process itself are quite simple but they are sufficiently abstract and subtle that they are often misunderstood. It may be easier to see the advantages of having prices equal marginal costs if we look at prices that persistently do not reflect marginal costs. We shall not consider a good or service that may benefit others besides the buyer, because pricing in such cases is more complicated. For example, the education of one person may benefit others; so as a matter of social policy the price of education might deliberately be subsidized to encourage more consumption by each of us. Assuming there is no such external benefit or cost, however, if the private decision of one consumer is based on that person paying less than cost, the final outcome will be both unfair and inefficient. It will be unfair because others must somehow bear the remaining cost of what this consumer buys. It will be inefficient because the cost of producing some units of the product will be higher than the value attached to them by the consumer.

Even if production costs at that output level are minimized, we must still label the result inefficient. The resources used to serve this consumer (who does not pay the resources' full cost) would be worth more to consumers elsewhere, where prices equal marginal costs. Obviously, the consumers would be willing to pay more (the full cost) for the resources there. Consumption goes beyond an optimal level when it is based on a price that misleads consumers by understating true cost.

When price remains above marginal cost the inefficiency that results is precisely the sort of inefficiency we associate with monopoly. At the value consumers place on the last unit of the good (value being represented by the price of the good), they do not consume as much of it as the society's resources and technology would allow them to consume. The consumers pay more than the value of resources needed to produce those marginal units while someone pockets the difference, and that can be unfair. Moreover, consumers are discouraged from consuming more even though they would place a greater value on any additional units than it would cost society to produce them; that is why, if this situation persists, we call it inefficient.

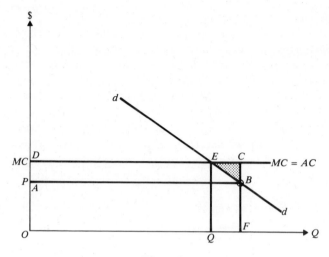

Figure 2.1

Figures 2.1 and 2.2 illustrate the effects of prices that do not equal marginal costs. Suppose the measures of quantities in the figures are defined for a specific time period such as a week, a day, or an hour. Marginal cost (*MC*) is constant regardless of output quantity, *Q*. The amount consumers are willing to pay to clear the market of any quantity is represented by the downward sloping linear demand curve, *dd*. In Figure 2.1 the price is *below* marginal cost; consumers pay the amount represented by the area *ABFO*, whereas total cost is the larger amount *DCFO*. The difference represented by *DCBA* is a transfer from somewhere else to these consumers. Notice that every unit of output beyond the point *E* is valued by consumers along demand curve *dd* at less than marginal cost. In going beyond point *E*, the difference between marginal cost and the lower valuation by consumers is captured by the triangle *ECB*. In Figure 2.2 the price is *above* marginal cost; consumers pay the amount represented by the area *ABFO*, whereas total cost is the smaller amount *DCFO*. Now the consumers give to the seller *ABCD*. Up to the output *E*, every unit that was not produced was valued more by consumers, as revealed by the demand curve, than it would have cost. Thus an amount of benefit represented by *ECB* is being lost as long as the price is held above marginal cost.

WHAT WILL MONOPOLY DO?

Prices that differ from marginal cost are to be expected in a dynamic competitive economy, but as long as resources can be attracted where there are

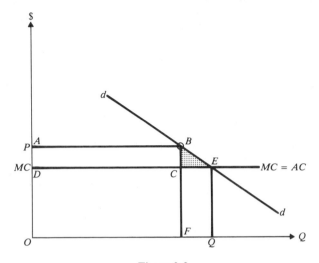

Figure 2.2

profits, or repelled where there are losses, the prices will be returned to marginal cost levels. Monopoly power can prevent resources from going where profits are high, and so it interferes with this competitive market adjustment. A monopoly might buy up all potential competitors or maintain excess capacity to discourage any new entrant. Or perhaps a seller may try to use *exclusive-requirements* contracts that bind customers over an extended period (for example, a contract requiring that all requirements for a certain service be provided by Company X), so for at least a limited time the customers are "captive."

The crucial question to ask is: how long can the monopoly advantage be sustained? Some economists argue that although monopoly control may be observed at any one time it will not persist, because as long as resources can be bought and sold the high profit of a monopolist will attract entrepreneurs ingenious enough to share in it [5, 6]. Others argue that such a process of new entry will take time and those attempting entry can face obstacles in their paths, perhaps even unfairly placed there by the monopolist [1, 4]. How long the market process should be left on its own to erode monopoly advantage is one question we shall face repeatedly, for it is at the heart of the question whether government should intervene to support competition. There is certainly more of a competitive threat in the market process over a long-run time period than there is in the short-run when few resources can be shifted from one activity to another. But it is difficult to judge just exactly how long a monopoly advantage will be sustained if no action is taken against it by government.

Once a monopoly can prevent new entry into its line of business it may do several things besides setting its price persistently above marginal cost. Rather than charge all consumers the same high price it may charge one consumer one price and another consumer another price, even though the cost of serving each consumer is the same. This is the practice called *price discrimination*. When charging only a single price the monopolist must lower it to sell more units, giving up some of the revenue on sales that were being made before the price was reduced. But a seller that can discriminate in price can keep the price higher to consumers who are willing to pay more while setting a lower price for those consumers who are only willing to pay less. By winning the business of both customer groups at different prices, the monopolist obviously can make more profit than by charging everyone the same price. But discrimination in price can work only if the product or service cannot easily be resold (like medical care), for trading of units among consumers would lead again to a single market price.

One interesting point about price discrimination is that although it will cause a transfer of income from consumers to the monopolist it need not interfere terribly with economic efficiency. When those charged high prices are willing to pay them, while those willing to pay only low prices are charged low prices down to the level of marginal cost, the efficiency of consumption choices is not seriously distorted. The last units purchased may be valued at close to their marginal cost. Indeed, price discrimination is actually a very efficient way to raise revenue. That is why some regulated public utilities are allowed to use price discrimination, by charging users of small amounts higher rates, when marginal cost is below average cost and pricing at marginal cost alone would lead to deficits.

A monopolist can force the consumer to buy another product (or products) that is *tied* to the monopolized one; in order to receive product A, say, you must also buy product B. If the tied product B is a supply item for the monopolized product, such as tabulating cards for use with a computer, a high price for the tied supply will bring a greater total payment from those with the most intense demand. Thus, the tying of the supply item actually can accomplish a form of price discrimination because those who value the service more presumably will use it more, and pay a higher effective price as a result. The monopolist also can gain advantages over other sellers in markets for the tied products, so the tying practice can be unfair to those sellers, too.

Having a monopoly position itself is so attractive it can invite a self-defeating form of competition in the effort to achieve it [6, pp. 8-15]. For instance, several different parties may try to invent a patentable product. Or several firms may try to gain a dominant position in a new field by growing, merging, and if possible obstructing others, expecting to be able to maintain the dominance once it is achieved, in part through advantages established sellers are expected to have over new ones. This kind of effort, predicated on the expectation of monopoly profit later, can sometimes create a race-like atmosphere during the developmental stages of a market. The consumers may benefit from ensuing innovations, but without them the effort to obtain monopoly will be socially wasteful.

Lacking pressure from competing producers once it is established, a monopoly may not keep its costs low. There are many stories of once-monopoly organizations, swollen with incompetent workers (maybe relatives of the boss) and saddled with poor investments or other management mistakes, that finally fail. The very protection monopolists enjoy from the intrusion of new methods and ideas can leave them unchallenged, and as a result they may go soft. Indeed, a traditional concern about government is based on this same prospect; since a government agency has monopoly power there is reason to question how efficiently it will be managed.

From medieval times the best of all monopoly positions has been that enforced by the power of government [4]. Questions about the efficiency of postal service, the army, or the county highway department arise too often to be entirely without merit. In the private sector telephone companies, television networks, railroads, airlines, trucking companies, and electric and gas companies, to name a few, are regulated with debatable effectiveness while being protected from new competition through exclusive certification procedures. National defense industries, those involved in foreign trade, the maritime industries, and others, have also benefited from large outright subsidies. American merchant vessels have been heavily subsidized by Congress, which often pays almost half the cost of building ships and more than half the cost of operating them, while the shipping companies are nevertheless failing to compete effectively for international shipping. Thus the monopoly power of government can be used to protect and sustain a failure as easily as an excessively profitable situation.

Even when a product market is under monopolistic control, some pressure for efficient operation of an unregulated private firm can arise through the capital market, where ownership shares in the firm are traded. On recognizing inefficient operations an investor may try to buy enough shares of the laggard firm to gain influence and sack its management, because by returning it to efficient operation the investor can enjoy a gain on the value of shares. But operations have to reach a sorry state to motivate such action and it is always risky. A successful raid to gain control of a sizeable corporation may require a vast sum of money and, even if control is achieved, it is not a simple matter to find the sources of inefficiencies and cure them. Lack of good information may also keep an investor from knowing of the opportunity to improve earnings in the first place. So without competition in the product market there is no guarantee that a product will be produced by the most efficient means available.

WHEN CAN COMPETITION WORK?

One would think from this brief review of competition and monopoly that our antitrust laws simply should insist on competition in markets and deny all monopoly. But the production technology best suited for some lines of business may not support competition. Firms may experience economies as they grow large relative to the total market for their product. Then, if all the firms are to operate at efficient sizes, there may be room for only a few firms in the market and entry will be difficult, a situation called *oligopoly*. A few firms in a market are able to see the effects their actions have on one another so they may depart from strict competitive behavior to be more co-operative.

To take an example, it has been estimated that to reach an efficient scale in automobile production a firm must approach nearly 10 percent of the to-tal U. S. market [1], which means that if each firm just reached that size there would be room for little more than 10 firms in the industry. That is a far cry from the very many sellers a perfectly competitive market calls for, and which most industries can accommodate [1, 7, 8]. Of course some auto firms in the United States are larger than the minimum-efficient size since we have only four domestic producers and they serve roughly three-fourths of the U. S. market.

There is another way in which great scale economies can limit the possi-bilities for competition. Unlike the perfectly competitive case, where a new firm can enter with scarcely any effect on market price, a newly entering firm that must increase industry output by 5 percent or 10 percent to reach efficient size surely will have to anticipate the effect its entry will have on market price. The potential entrant might judge that to win an adequate share of the market it will have to force price down by, say, 5 percent, so the firm will not even attempt entry unless the market price is about 5 percent above the level at which it can make a reasonable profit. The high price that will stimulate entry is sometimes called a *limit price*, for the reason that it is an upper limit on prices the existing firms can charge without inviting new entry.

In these circumstances low transportation costs may enlarge the sizes of markets, and international trade may enforce competition. Many countries have a domestic market so small they cannot support a single automobile producer, but producers from other countries will compete for their busi-ness as long as no one has a commanding advantage in transportation cost. Thus, when the techniques of production offer significant economies of large scale so only a small number of efficient-sized suppliers exist in one country, tariff policies and transportation costs can become crucial in deter-mining whether competition will function reliably.

When knowledge is not magically complete for us all, and especially when dynamic possibilities such as technological change are to be considered, we may not favor competition unambiguously on efficiency grounds, either. For example, as new ideas are discovered technology can be altered to lower costs of old products or to bring new products into existence; thus, an incentive for developing new ideas is worth consideration. Restriction of competition has been adopted for this very purpose in the form of the *patent* award, which creates a property right for the inventor in the use of a new idea.

A patent was first offered by the Republic of Venice in 1474. Today the U. S. patent award gives the inventor a monopoly right lasting seventeen years, a compromise between the two alternative periods, fourteen years and twenty-one years, chosen in England to allow training through the apprentice system of either two or three sets of workmen under the new technique. But the initial monopolist often can find patentable improvements that extend effective monopoly control much longer. Originally intended to benefit the individual inventor, and to this day awarded only to individuals, the patent has come increasingly to be controlled by corporations. At the turn of the century over three-fourths of patent rights were retained by individuals whereas today almost three-fourths are assigned instead to organizations. Large organizations have even joined in cross-licensing agreements within their industries, under which they share ideas to exploit them more than they could have separately.

It is difficult to see what balance to strike with patents, to decide how much protection they should allow and for how long a time period. Surveys show them to be important incentives now for firms in some industries such as drugs and electronics, but unimportant in others. They seem to be less important as an incentive to larger firms than smaller ones. We can say they help to encourage inventive activity, but to offset that benefit is a social cost in the excess of price over cost that marks monopoly pricing of a product. The presence in the economy of legitimate monopoly power based on patents also makes it more difficult for antitrust authorities to recognize illegal monopoly actions for what they are.[3] Still, an inventor's right to an idea seems to deserve protection, and patents probably will exist to create monopoly advantages for a long time to come. Those industries in which patents are important also are often the most dynamic and innovative in the economy.

Lack of information by consumers can be a source of antitrust problems. Seeking hotel accommodation in an unfamiliar town or shopping for a new or used car will quickly convince you that we are not always well informed about products and services we might buy. When there is ignorance there may be shoddy goods and sellers may attempt misleading representations, for when such acts can be profitable someone in a community may be tempted to engage in them. Acts to mislead need to be dealt with if competition is to work well, not only to ensure fairness but also in order that individuals have enough confidence to deal with one another in markets.

By being known to its regular customers, an already existing seller can enjoy a slight monopoly position over those of its customers who do not know about alternative sources of supply. A new retail shop or a new product may not attract consumers because the consumers never learn of it. Advertising informs consumers, of course, but it will not always move the world closer to the perfectly competitive ideal because advertising by established firms actually can make it more difficult for a new firm to be heard. Furthermore, advertising is not always informative. Some advertising makes only vague claims, providing nothing so specific as a price or a technical detail about the product advertised. Advertising also can have effects beyond product markets; despite handsome earnings prospects, a young firm may not find it easy to raise funds in capital markets because investors have never heard of it. Moreover, the efforts of large advertisers might be more effective per dollar than those of small advertisers, either because one brand name can be advertised to enhance many of a large firm's products at once, or because the rates charged to large advertisers are lower. Thus advertising as a source of information may add to the economies of large-scale operation that make it harder for competition to work.

Large firms that operate in many industries may appear to investors almost as mutual funds because they are so diversified that some activities will yield good profits while others have poor profits, leaving some average level of profit reliably available at low risk. Holding shares in that one firm saves the investor the brokerage fees and the attention needed to maintain a portfolio of less diversified firms. If investors value more highly the shares of large diversified firms as a result, that will lower the cost of capital for them. At the same time, the large diversified firm may also offer more effective supervision of its separate divisions than the capital market would provide, so the result may be more efficient [9]. Thus, another economy of large scale may follow from the presence of risks and the brokerage costs of transactions in capital markets; the large scale may allow more effective management of separate enterprises than the capital market would enforce.

Thus the smooth functioning of competition is not always feasible, however convinced we might be of its virtues under the right circumstances. There are problems of technology, where the efficient scale of production works against having many competitors, and advantages in yielding to monopoly where new ideas are to be encouraged. There are other problems caused by lack of knowledge and information and by uncertainty. In part because these problems of competition's feasibility are so serious, our public officials have been reluctant to rely thoroughly on competition and there is considerable disagreement over the role competition may play in antitrust policy today. In addition, the possession by large corporations of elements of political power limits the aims one can expect for antitrust policy.

ANTITRUST AIMS

To assess the limitations we just discussed and to describe real world markets, a framework has been developed that focuses on operational measures of important industry characteristics. These characteristics include (1) the ease of entry into an industry; (2) the number of firms in the industry or some other such measure of how much the industry's decisions are concentrated in a few hands; (3) the extent to which products are differentiated from one another by design, advertising, or other selling methods; (4) the price elasticity of market demand, meaning the extent to which price changes cause quantity changes; and (5) the way total costs of firms respond to changes in outputs. Such characteristics are called elements of *market structure* and they are expected to be linked to market conduct and finally to the market's economic performance. If such a connection can be established it can of course help policy makers see how to induce better industry performance.

The market structure measures are intended to capture in an objective way some of the variety that is found in real world industries. They have been chosen because of their expected influence on how firms in an industry will behave. Price setting, advertising, research and development, and other decisions by firms comprise market conduct. For example, if new entrants cannot easily intrude because barriers exist, and firms already in an industry are few enough to be able to agree, perhaps tacitly, then prices are apt to be higher. The extent of product differentiation, the elasticity of demand, and cost function properties can all affect the payoffs to firms for alternative price and advertising actions in such situations. We shall consider this industrial organization framework in more detail in Chapter 5, when we try to evaluate the actual performance of industries. For now, we want to focus on just what the final goals of antitrust policy might be, to see what good performance would mean.

By considering a simple representation of a market economy it is easy enough to see a role for *efficiency* as a goal; the issue of fairness or *equity* also can be defined and pursued as a goal in such a framework. With complications like economies of scale, technical progress, imperfect information and risk, however, the question of social aims becomes more complex. Provision should now be made for technical *progress* as a goal; further, some provision should also be made to keep the economy *stable* so resources can by *fully employed*. Efficiency becomes more complicated when economies of scale exist. If the economies of scale are very great, a more efficient result may be obtained by forgoing competition and operating only one or a few firms in the industry. Equity will become a more complicated aim, too, because in addition to income distribution questions a host of difficult fairness questions can arise when imperfect information is present as well as monopoly.

It still seems entirely reasonable to pursue competitive organization of markets, as long as doing so will not require that firms be held to such a small size they will forgo significant scale economies [3]. However, under democratic political institutions debate can be expected over such a goal, especially if some firms already hold strong market positions. Scale economies are not easy to measure accurately so it is hard to settle empirically the question of their importance. Indeed, if the power that accompanies market control can be used to improve a firm's profit rate a dominant firm may make itself *look* more efficient. Certainly the dominant firms in a market would argue they were more efficient to Congress. And the truth may not always be revealed through debate when all facts cannot be known.

Entry to an industry may be difficult because of scale economies and because new entrants cannot easily inform customers and investors about the opportunities they offer. But there is no ready and cost-free cure for imperfect information, and the technology that allows scale economies usually cannot be changed. It may simply be impossible to create a competitive environment by policy action. Yet when monopoly develops, some effort will be needed to contain its most obvious abuses. Any one situation may call for subtle economic diagnosis, and to give fair treatment any resulting policy action should be based on rules that can be applied uniformly.

Thus efficiency is not easy to pursue directly. As a goal it can conflict with reasonable incentives to achieve progressiveness. An example is awarding a patent that may elicit desired inventive activity but will also tend to use the invention inefficiently by allowing its monopolization. Equity may stand in the way of efficiency, too, if efficiency requires changing a well-established property right. The aims of full employment and stability are less obviously in conflict with efficiency but they also are not always easily achieved. And of course any legislation, including antitrust legislation, may reflect the selfish purposes of certain legislators rather than the lofty goals a whole society might ideally set for itself.

In Chapter 5 we shall return to these questions of industry structure and conduct and to the problem of defining good performance. But first we must turn to the antitrust laws themselves, and probe into their enactment and enforcement. For the laws and the way they are enforced ought to influence the structure, conduct, and ultimate performance of industry.

SUMMARY

Under ideal conditions competition might control our economic affairs well, reward effort fairly, and ensure efficient production of those goods consumers wanted. This potentially marvelous social institution is handicapped, however, by imperfections in the world. For low-cost operation, technology can sometimes require that producers have a substantial fraction of the sales in their markets, for instance, and that requirement can lead in turn to an equilibrium in which there are too few firms to support competition. How can antitrust authorities insist on competitive behavior in a market with only three or four firms, where competitive behavior is not really well defined? Furthermore, no government policy can alter the technical conditions that require large scale for most efficient operations.

Another problem is allowing incentives for the discovery of new products and techniques of production. One solution is to rely on the award of a patent monopoly as incentive, even though doing so can complicate control of monopoly in the economy. We also have imperfections in the information each of us has. Even though markets can economize on the need for information by relying on prices to guide decentralized choices, those choices may not be fully informed ones, and the consequences that follow may be unfair. Existing firms can benefit from imperfect information because it handicaps new producers in reaching consumers, and of course consumers can be cheated even more directly, by misleading claims and faulty products. On the other hand, no cure is readily available, because making us all perfectly informed would cost far too much (if it were even feasible). Although deliberate deception may be punished, lack of complete information is apt to be a continuing problem.

Under such circumstances we must forgo absolutes and might pursue as reasonable the social goals of efficiency, progressiveness, equity, and full employment and stability. But such goals cannot all be pursued at once, for many policies may allow progress toward one goal and make more difficult the accomplishment of another. Even in attempting to approximate a competitive standard where it might be feasible, the realities of political power will not always allow a sound economic solution to a problem. Equipped with knowledge of the benefits competition can offer, but mindful of the technical and political obstacles in attempting to realize them, let us now begin our study of the American attempt to preserve some of these benefits of competition.

REFERENCES

1. Joe S. Bain. *Barriers to New Competition.* Cambridge, Mass.: Harvard University Press, 1956.

2. Ward S. Bowman, Jr. *Patent and Antitrust Law.* Chicago, Ill.: University of Chicago Press, 1973.

3. Kenneth G. Elzinga. "The Goals of Antitrust: Other than Competition and Efficiency, What Else Counts." *University of Pennsylvania Law Review* 125: 1191-1213 (June 1977).

4. Mark J. Green, ed. *The Monopoly Makers*. New York: Grossman, 1973.

5. Israel Kirzner. *Competition and Entrepreneurship*. Chicago, Ill.: University of Chicago Press, 1973.

6. Richard Posner. *Antitrust Law: An Economic Perspective*. Chicago, Ill.: Unisity of Chicago Press, 1976.

7. F. Michael Scherer, *et al. The Economics of Multi-Plant Operation*. Cambridge, Mass.: Harvard University Press, 1975.

8. Roger Sherman. *The Economics of Industry*. Boston, Mass.: Little, Brown and Co., 1974.

9. Oliver E. Williamson, *Corporate Control and Business Behavior*. Englewood Cliffs, N. J.: Prentice-Hall, 1970.

END NOTES

1. *U. S.* v. *S. E. Underwriters Assn.*, 322 U. S. 533, 559 (1944).

2. The value of all resources needed to produce each of the last, or marginal, units is also called the *marginal cost*. Marginal cost at a given output level thus represents the change in total cost caused by the production of one more unit of output.

3. For examination of patent policies in the context of antitrust policy see [2].

The Coming of   3
Antitrust Law

Out of the great expansion in economic activity that followed the Civil War there emerged large combinations of firms within many industries called trusts after the voting trusts that appeared in the 1880s. Reports about ruthless abuse of the growing power of trusts were legend. Yet they could not be controlled at common law because their actions were not unambiguous offenses. Under such circumstances, with little economic knowledge to draw on and with conflicting interests to be reconciled, Congress passed the Sherman Act to initiate antitrust economic policy in America.

But business combinations continued to be formed. The Sherman Act was more an expression of sentiment for an objective than a clear instruction for reaching it, and it was slow to have effect. In 1914, after the Sherman Act began to take hold, the Clayton and Federal Trade Commission Acts were passed because the Sherman Act alone was thought inadequate to achieve its purpose. These later modifications contained no startling new initiative or abrupt change of direction, however, and antitrust law today remains the product of late Victorian America. That is why an understanding of the antitrust laws currently in use requires an appreciation of the turn-of-the-century attitudes and circumstances that prompted their enactment.

The common law background of antitrust will be sketched first, to be followed by a brief portrait of turn-of-the-century America. Then three separate sections will be devoted to the Sherman Act, the Clayton and Federal Trade Commission Acts, and other developments since those major laws were passed.

COMMON LAW BACKGROUND FOR ANTITRUST

Framers of the Sherman Act claimed they were merely codifying common law, and early antitrust cases drew on it. But the common law of late medieval England covered so many offenses in commerce, changed so often, and was so inconsistent, that it is probably wrong to think of it as providing any very clear basis for modern antitrust policy.[1] The word *monopoly* was not even used until the sixteenth century and early offenses were more often threats against established economic power than abuses of it. The circumstances of the common law offenses were also very different from those of the antitrust era.

The earliest economic offenses at common law, for example, the so-called middleman offenses in England, represent no harbinger of modern antitrust policy. They reveal better the great contrast between modern and medieval times. These offenses grew partly out of a medieval belief (rarely expressed today because commerce is now so well accepted) that middlemen perform no useful function. Buying goods before they could come to market (sometimes buying crops before they were harvested) or generally buying in bulk to resell in smaller quantities was indictable at common law in the thirteenth century. The dominant business unit of that day was the guild, a professional trade and even social organization dating back to Roman times. A guild often had rights to hold markets, granted as royal franchises by the Crown, and to protect them they prosecuted middlemen. The prosecutions declined as town markets gave way to national markets in England, where middlemen were more obviously useful, and middlemen offenses were never important in the United States.

Antimonopoly actions closer to modern antitrust efforts go back to the end of the sixteenth century in England when the great power of guilds, and also of the Crown, was slipping while Parliament and the common law were becoming more important. A famous example is the *Case of Monopolies*[2] in 1603 in which an importer of playing cards was sued because Queen Elizabeth had granted her groom the sole right to import playing cards into England. The court held this grant of a playing-card monopoly void, saying it was counter to common law. Grants of monopoly were being seen more and more as harming actual and potential competitors by their advantages in winning business, and harming the public through higher prices and poorer quality. Monopoly was not being rejected, though. It was the acts of some monopolists, not the fact of their holding monopoly positions, that was rejected at common law.

In 1623 Parliament went further and passed the Statute of Monopolies to void all monopolies, a statute that was studied carefully by framers of the Sherman Act. The Statute of Monopolies cannot be seen as a sharp turning point in antimonopoly history, however, for its effective use against monopolies was to come many years later. For one thing, it preserved as exceptions Parliamentary grants of monopoly, patents, and the monopolies held by towns or guilds to control trading. So a very large share of economic activity was still governed by monopoly organization. Furthermore, England was moving toward a political revolution in which the members of Parliament would oppose the king. The Statute of Monopolies (along with other statutes) could not be uniformly effective while its legitimacy was in doubt.[3]

It is true that conspiracies of several persons for an unlawful purpose frequently were broken down at common law. But to be found unlawful the conspiracies had either to use unlawful means or to seek a goal that was counter to the public interest, and those terms were not treated in a very consistent way. In the United States, common law conspiracy doctrines were applied mainly to labor union activities, although combinations of corporations to restrict competition were also forbidden early in a few states. Workers who joined labor unions in England were challenged as conspirators until late in the nineteenth century when the British Parliament reformed labor law.

Even restrictions on trade that existed at the time were not opposed consistently at common law. For instance, before 1700 in England a contract that would have the seller of a business restrained (in some region and for some time period) from competing against the buyer of his business might not be enforced, usually on the ground that one with a trade or skill should not be kept from using it; but by about 1700 such contracts came to be respected as long as they were freely joined into and were deemed reasonable, either for the parties or for the public. Indeed, the parties themselves were often regarded as the best judges of reasonableness, and English courts were even known to uphold price-fixing agreements as reasonable contracts! Courts in America were not so blind to the public interest—that is, the interest of those who were not party to the agreement but who were nevertheless affected by it—although decisions varied considerably from one state to another.

As we have noted, with the eighteenth and nineteenth centuries came economic change on a scale never before experienced, a transition to modern life appropriately called the industrial revolution. In England during this period legislative statutes came to supersede much of the common law precedent. There was the Statute of Monopolies to use against monopolies, where the common law had grown particularly weak; the Trade Union Acts to supersede common law against combinations of workers; and an abolition of common law against forestalling, a form of middleman offense related to monopoly pricing. Only for restraint of trade was the common law relevant, and there it was not applied consistently. Although English common law was relied on to some extent in America in the late 1800s it still cannot be claimed that common law provided a firm foundation for the Sherman Act.

TURN-OF-THE-CENTURY AMERICA

There were some electric lights but no neon signs or television in 1890; indeed, the first radio signal was sent by Marconi in 1895. That was also the year celluloid film was first employed as a vehicle for moving pictures, but successful combination with recorded voice into "talking pictures" was years away. There was no miracle medicine of today, despite the zany claims made for patent medicines, produced largely from alcohol, that were being peddled. Although railroads were sweeping westward, most transportation (other than by foot) was by water or horse. The horse imparted an odor (and flies) to urban life that would be unthinkable today. Cities were growing but did not yet have skyscrapers, for architecture was only beginning to follow the forms that steel and glass later would allow. The nation was agrarian, individualistic, even entrepreneurial, without the European feudal tradition and without the entrenched and symbolically reinforced economic and political power of European nation states. It is not surprising then that we were drawn into something of an economic free-for-all.

The end of the Civil War in America had ushered in a period of truly dramatic economic growth.[4] Between the Civil War and 1900, 14 million immigrants swelled the American work force, and more land was settled than in all the time since the continent had been discovered. Railroads laced western settlements together in economic activity with the East. A national banking system was established that helped firms raise capital and grow to serve emerging national markets. It was in this period that the corporate form of business organization spread from canals and railroads to industry and commerce generally.

Along with its benefits, the rapid economic development of the late 1800s brought oppression to the underprivileged and scandal among the privileged. City dwellers, including children, worked long hours in dirty, poorly lit, and unsafe places, and that working life was not relieved by the slum conditions endured at home. Labor and local businesses both fell under the power of corporations in trusts and combinations that grew steadily more powerful, often by forcing competitors to sell out under the threat of ruin. City officials who gave out valuable lighting, water, street railway, and other contracts were bribed routinely. Western farmers felt they were suffering from the steadily falling price level and the growing power of railroads and industries. Stock prices were manipulated in merger schemes as trusts and combinations proliferated. Trust stood for monopoly, and in America this is the period that gave monopoly its bad name.

How to remedy this trust problem was not at all obvious, particularly to Congressmen who shared private business sympathies and to a public that believed in private enterprise. Many states had adopted antimonopoly constitutional provisions or statutes but, with a few exceptions, they did not enforce them. State attorneys general lacked resources; even where they had them they were naturally reluctant to drive large employers from their states. Courts also limited the actions that could be taken against corporations when they treated the corporations as persons and extended to them due process protections. So the combinations continued.

After the Civil War there began a remarkable battle for control of railroads that illustrates the excesses of the trust movement.[5] Daniel Drew, the Great Bear who ran the Erie Railroad, was joined by James Fisk and Jay Gould in a struggle against the New York Central Railroad headed by Commodore Vanderbilt and, later, J. Pierpont Morgan. Vanderbilt bought Erie Railroad shares because that railroad was a potential competitor for his own designs on a route to Chicago; he learned only later that Drew was selling vast numbers of shares, some of them illegally, and also was increasing the indebtedness of Erie to purchase at vastly inflated prices certain properties Drew himself owned. After a brief truce this battle broke out again as both sides used decisions by judges to help them in turn-by-turn legal ploys. At one point Jay Gould spread an estimated one million dollars around the New York State legislature seeking helpful law making. Similar battles accompanied a race for control of railroads to the West. Collis Huntington in California and the Southwest and James J. Hill in the Northwest won substantial regional control although skirmishing continued. In the East, where Drew held the Erie while Vanderbilt controlled the New York Central they faced as rivals the Pennsylvania and the Baltimore and Ohio railroads. J. P. Morgan worked for cooperation nationwide but encountered repeated difficulties, especially from the head of the Illinois Central Railroad, Edward H. Harriman. These early leaders played a sophisticated version of the present-day Monopoly board game, but although they were charged frequently with illegal acts they seldom went to jail.

In 1887 Congress created the Interstate Commerce Commission (the ICC) to regulate railroad power. The ICC was the first of our federal administrative agencies, which are part legislative, part executive, and part judicial. Whether the railroads actually favored the creation of this commission so competition could be better controlled is still debated, for it was not resisted by them uniformly.[6] Meanwhile, not far behind the railroads in ruthlessness were efforts of small groups of individuals to control meat, oil, tobacco, steel, sugar, lead, whiskey, gun powder, and other industries. There was no clamor from the public for antitrust legislation because it was not obvious that legislation could solve the problem.

THE SHERMAN ACT AND ITS EARLY ENFORCEMENT

The initiative for a new federal law to deal with trusts came from President Harrison, who won election in 1888 claiming the Republicans would find ways to compel competition while at the same time raising protective tariffs. Although a number of antimonopoly bills were introduced at Harrison's urging, his intent for this legislation seems to have been cosmetic, to make his tariff increases more acceptable to the public (the McKinley tariff of 1890 which Harrison favored expanded coverage and set high tariff rates, averaging 50 percent of the value of goods traded).

It is never easy to summarize all the conflicting intentions behind passage of a new law and to do so in the case of the Sherman Act would be almost impossible.[7] Here a problem was evident but the knowledge to understand and deal with it was not at hand. The law's namesake John Sherman was an aging and respected senator from Ohio who had almost become the Republican party's candidate instead of Harrison for the 1888 election. In addition to introducing his own bill he struggled mightily for two years to control investigation of the antitrust question, but was not entirely successful. Whether an antitrust law would be constitutional or whether it could be enforced were questions much debated, along with details such as what words to use to express violations of the law and how to penalize them. In the end a bill that had been entirely rewritten by the Judiciary Committee was readily adopted and named for Senator Sherman.

Many of the congressmen most active in the law's framing (in addition to Senator Sherman, Senators Edmunds of Vermont, Hoar of Massachusetts, and George of Mississippi, who were by no means alike in their proposals) claimed it to be an affirmation of an old common law doctrine, and an attempt had been made to express the act in language from common law. The framers even sketched the interpretation they placed on the common law [2] but no very exact meaning was then in use for the words adopted such as *trust, conspiracy, restraint of trade,* or *monopolize.*

Moreover, no potent remedy was created for violations of the act, nor were any new funds voted for the already overworked Department of Justice to see to its enforcement. One might suspect that the large firms that were to be subject to this new act had influenced it, at least in adding to its vagueness and lack of remedies. Legislators appear to have passed a difficult problem along to the courts while hoping at the same time to satisfy the voters' desire for action, because the Sherman Act was worded in very broad terms, almost like constitutional provisions, prohibiting restraint of trade and monopolization.

Section 1 of the act, as amended,[8] provides that

[e]very contract, combination in the form of trust or otherwise, or conspiracy, in restraint of trade or commerce among the several States, or with foreign nations, is declared to be illegal . . .

To prove a contract, combination, or conspiracy, some definite agreement must be found to exist among at least two parties, and that agreement must restrain trade unreasonably if it is to be judged illegal today. To be subject to the act the trade or commerce should involve parties from different states or foreign nations, but such involvement has been readily established for economic activity within a single city[9] if it significantly affects commerce between states.

Section 2 of the Act, as amended,[10] declares

> [e]very person who shall monopolize, or attempt to monopolize, or combine or conspire with any other person or persons, to monopolize any part of the trade or commerce among the several States, or with foreign nations, shall be deemed guilty of a felony . . .

Although no entirely unambiguous definition of monopoly yet exists, this section essentially prohibits any private party from having power to control price in a particular market or to prevent entry into it, where such power was sought or obtained by methods evidencing an intent to exercise it. In these sections the Sherman Act declared a national policy, but it left to the courts the task of determining the meaning of its prohibitions in specific application. We shall take up those applications in Chapter 4, when we examine the enforcement of the antitrust laws.

These Sherman Act provisions went beyond simple codification of existing common law. For one thing the act provided for private parties to bring civil suits against one another by granting to a successful plaintiff three times the extent of damages he suffered. This incentive to prosecute was expanded by the Antitrust Improvements Act of 1976,[11] which allowed state attorneys general to sue on behalf of residents and, if successful, to collect treble damages for the state. The Sherman Act also made some violations crimes, thereby enlisting the government's obligation to enforce it for society. This and subsequent legislation led to the creation of federal government agencies to pursue antitrust policy.

But only seven suits were instituted under the Sherman Act by President Harrison, eight by President Cleveland (in his second administration), and three by President McKinley. And these suits seemed utterly ineffective in slowing the trend to corporate consolidation and monopoly. In 1895, when the first Sherman Act case reached the Supreme Court, the formation of a sugar trust was not prevented.[12] And most of the successful cases prosecuted during President Cleveland's administration were against labor unions. Yet Congress did not amend the act. And there were more business combinations in the McKinley administration than ever before.

There are many reasons for the initial ineffectiveness of the Sherman Act against trusts. It is not easy to absorb a new legal jurisdiction and see exactly what cases should be brought under it. Moreover, the Department of Justice could not have moved at once on all potential Sherman Act fronts even if funds had been available or if the influential first attorney general under President Cleveland, Richard Olney, had been sympathetic to the act (which he was not). Politicians were distracted by many other important problems in these last years of the nineteenth century, including war with Spain. Many urged that a new navy be inaugurated. Clear pensions for war veterans were needed. Tariff policy was continually debated, for while high tariffs brought government revenue and benefited big business, the public objected to them. The national forests were being plundered. Indians were being cheated of their lands. The western states demanded the coining of silver, while issuing currency without backing in any rare metal was also debated. There was no sound system of taxation. And, in addition to outrageous business scandals, government corruption arose, for an enormous spoils system had developed in the national government. With all of these serious problems facing government, the economy faltered, and the last years of the century were economically depressed.

Just as the Sherman Act was passed to stop them the trusts were benefited by another development. Responding partly to a financial crisis, the state of New Jersey enacted an incorporation law that abandoned most of the restraints limiting corporation behavior. New Jersey also repealed its antitrust law. In effect, the state set out to make money by granting lenient corporate charters, and was so successful in attracting corporation filing fees and franchise taxes that in ten years it could pay off all its debt. New Jersey first allowed one corporation to own another, making the holding company legal, and later granted unlimited life and size to corporations, plus the use of financial instruments and devices that facilitated mergers. Since a firm incorporated in one state could operate in others, combinations essentially like trusts could become legal by incorporating in New Jersey. Of course many of the goals of a trust were now illegal because of the Sherman Act, but the trust's mere existence was no longer in violation of state incorporation statutes.

The foundation for antitrust action that was to come later lay quietly dormant in the seemingly harmless Sherman Act while district attorneys around the nation began to initiate investigations that would lead to prosecutions. Soon the act would alter radically the administration of law in matters concerning competition, now that divergent state rules were supported by a uniform federal law. More importantly, as we have noted already, restraining trade and monopolization were branded as crimes under the act, punishable as violations of the rules needed to maintain society. Private parties, either as individuals or as corporations, and in 1976 state governments as well, were given incentive to enforce the law because they could sue to recover treble the damages they suffered.

Before the end of the nineteenth century, as cases made their way on appeal to the Supreme Court, the Sherman Act began to have effects. In 1892 the government had sued the Trans-Missouri Freight Association, made up of fifteen railroads that controlled rail traffic west of the Mississippi, seeking its dissolution on the ground that as a combination fixing rates and setting uniform rules it violated Section 1 of the Sherman Act.[13] The association agreed it had formed for mutual protection by maintaining reasonable rates, rules, and regulations. It also claimed these activities were acceptable at common law, and that Section 1 prohibited only those restraints that had been held unlawful at common law. The Supreme Court, in an opinion written by Justice Peckham in 1897, found the association unlawful because Section 1 condemned *every* restraint of trade.

The ways in which restraints of trade had been handled at common law were considered carefully in the *Addyston Pipe and Steel* case, a price-fixing case decided in favor of the government by the Circuit Court of Appeals in 1898.[14] Defendants in the case were manufacturers and sellers of cast iron pipe who accounted for 65 percent of production capacity over roughly three-fourths of the United States. They argued that, although a committee of them fixed their price, they had to meet competitive prices since they did not control the whole market, so their final price was reasonable. In an immensely important decision for shifting attention to *market power* rather than *market conduct*, the court held that the agreement would be invalid at common law because it gave the parties *power* to charge unreasonable prices. Whether they charged unreasonable prices or not, the combination was condemned for its power.

These two decisions at the close of the nineteenth century fell like bombshells on the business community. The Sherman Act had teeth after all, at least in the area of price-fixing. Businessmen were dismayed; they resented this intrusion into their affairs and feared an even more general breach of the private enterprise faith. It was not that businessmen resisted change, for one new technology was being discovered after another, with chemicals perhaps leading the way, and industrial research laboratories were already making their appearance [10]. Tall commercial buildings of steel and glass also were starting to mark the major cities. But at the same time the accumulation of economic power finally was being restrained.

Theodore Roosevelt became president in 1901, when President McKinley was struck down by an anarchist's bullet. A self-proclaimed red-blooded American, Roosevelt urged in his first message to Congress about twenty-five reforms, including regulation of trusts, railroads, and banks. He was responding to a growing public concern. Under increasingly lenient state incorporation laws, trusts continued to be formed at a rapid rate, largely through the efforts of certain large insurance companies and great banking houses, such as J. P. Morgan's, in New York City. They worked to form trusts and combinations because the manipulation of share values commonly allowed promoters to gain handsomely.

President Roosevelt turned his great energy to the antitrust problem. He quickly formed the Department of Commerce and recommended that it study corporations. The resulting examination of the conduct of interstate corporations furnished material for important antitrust cases in oil, steel, tobacco, and other industries. For the first time, resources were deliberately set aside for antitrust enforcement. In 1902 Roosevelt's attorney general[15] proceeded against a giant railway consolidation that would have brought Hill, Morgan, and Harriman together in what is known as the *Northern Securities* case.[16] And in 1904, by a five to four vote, the Court enjoined the holding company in the *Northern Securities* case from exercising control over competing railroads and did not let the railroads pay dividends to the holding company. That decision came as another big shock to Wall Street. Banker J. P. Morgan and businessman Mark Hanna had attempted personally to intercede with the president but the decision stood.

The antitrust movement really seemed to bloom in 1911 when the Supreme Court found the Standard Oil Company an illegal monopoly under Section 2 of the Sherman Act.[17] The firm had come to dominate domestic oil production and distribution, and it left behind a trail of mergers and consolidations often coerced by economic power. Indeed, its viscious and oppressive tactics against numerous competitors revealed unmistakably that its goal had been monopoly. It ran afoul of the Sherman Act at almost every turn, and the record of its actions remains today an excellent example of ruthlessly monopolistic behavior [18]. Chief Justice White, in stating the Court's opinion, expressed the illegality of the actions clearly enough but he went further to set out a reasonableness test that came to be called the *rule of reason*. Under this principle it was not enough to be a monopoly or to attempt to be a monopoly; to be illegal a firm also had to behave *unreasonably*. Standard Oil had behaved unreasonably, and in the Court's opinion it was this unreasonable behavior that led to its conviction.

Chief Justice White had favored this reasonableness requirement earlier (he had dissented in the 1897 *Trans-Missouri Freight Association* case mentioned above, and in similar cases). A basis for his position could be found in the common law, where precedents actually had made illegal only the *unreasonable* restraints of trade and the monopolies *contrary to the public interest*. But of course as it was written the Sherman Act had no such qualification. Indeed, it explicitly opposed *every* restraint of trade and *every* monopoly. Thus by introducing the rule of reason and looking to market conduct rather than to the possession of market power alone, the Court now seemed to be in conflict with the intentions of the Congress.

THE CLAYTON AND FEDERAL TRADE COMMISSION ACTS

Many congressmen disliked the rule of reason because of its apparent swerving away from the stated Sherman Act goal of opposing *every* monopoly and restraint of trade, whether reasonable or not. This feeling, together with the reforming efforts of President Woodrow Wilson, led in 1914 to the enactment of the Clayton Act and the Federal Trade Commission Act.[18] The Clayton Act could be seen as an effort to define unreasonable behavior more specifically to make it easier to prove, thereby harnessing the rule of reason to good effect. Even as it was passed, though, the Clayton Act was regarded by many to be a weak law, because it was a compromise between those seeking detailed specification of offenses and those wanting generality.

The Clayton Act is more specific than the Sherman Act in making particular business practices unlawful, not for causing monopoly with certainty, but rather where the effect of these business practices could "substantially lessen competition or tend to create a monopoly in any line of commerce." Section 2 of the Clayton Act, which was amended by the Robinson-Patman Act in 1936 and is now identical with that act's first section, prohibits discrimination in price.[19] As noted in Chapter 2, price discrimination occurs whenever different prices are charged to different customers for the same good (or, conceivably, where the same price is charged for different goods). Under Section 2 it is unlawful to discriminate in price among those who purchase goods of like grade and quality in interstate or foreign commerce where the effect "may be substantially to lessen competition or tend to create a monopoly in any line of commerce, or to injure, destroy, or prevent competition with any person who knowingly receives the benefit of such discrimination, or with customers of either of them."

Added provisions of Section 2 allow some scope for different prices to different customers if they can be justified by cost differences, or if the lower price is undertaken in good faith to meet the equally low price of a competitor. Further subsections of the act control brokerage payments that may be part of the price and the use of promotional services or facilities; these are major alternative ways of altering effective prices or costs so buyers and sellers might achieve the main aims of price discrimination without appearing to use it. Although this section of the act can prevent some very unfair pricing practices, it has been most troublesome in application. Largely because of its great concern for *injury to competitors*, which can follow of course from genuine competition without really harming the process of competition itself, its sanctions have inhibited genuine competitive behavior.

Section 3 of the Clayton Act prohibits anticompetitive *exclusive-dealing* arrangements, *total-requirement* obligations, and *tying*, whether in sale or lease arrangements.[20] Exclusive dealing commits a purchaser to buy from a single supplier and no others; total-requirement contracts have the same effect of obliging a buyer to use the same source of supply over the period of a contract, whatever the buyer's needs may be. With tying contracts one or more goods would be made available for sale only on the condition that another good or goods also be purchased. When used by one firm these practices can deny its competitors access to potential customers. As with other parts of the act, these practices are unlawful only where their probable effect "may be substantially to lessen competition or to tend to create a monopoly."

Section 7 of the Clayton Act deals with corporate acquisitions and mergers. It was amended importantly in 1950 by the Celler-Kefauver Act to define mergers more carefully and to include mergers effected through the sale of assets rather than the sale of stock shares alone. Under this law one corporation cannot acquire another "where in any line of commerce in any section of the country, the effect of such acquisition may be substantially to lessen competition, or to tend to create a monopoly."[21] With the tightening of this proscription in 1950 almost all mergers among competing firms of significant size—called horizontal mergers—have been eliminated, so that most of the remaining mergers since 1950 are among firms not related as direct rivals, the so-called conglomerate mergers involving firms that are not in competing product lines. One of the provisions of the Antitrust Improvements Act of 1976 requires that large firms notify the government in advance of any merger with another firm, so the government can act against it more effectively if it wishes.

As it turned out, the antimerger provisions (Section 7) did not cover anticompetitive acquisition if accomplished through outright purchase of assets rather than purchase of stock shares, so it was not fully effective until amended in 1950 by the Celler-Kefauver Act. The Clayton Act's sanctions against price discrimination were altered in 1936 by the Robinson-Patman Act. Its sanctions against tying and exclusive dealing were effective, and the act outlawed interlocking directorates beyond certain sizes in corporations and banks. It contained provisions that made officers of corporations personally responsible for violations of the law, but the provisions failed when the government could not win early cases under them. The act did clarify one thing: it exempted labor unions from the antitrust laws.

The Federal Trade Commission Act, passed in 1914 and amended in 1938, 1973, and 1975, set up a nonpartisan commission of five members appointed for seven-year terms by the president to interpret and enforce its provisions, subject to review by courts. Unfair methods of competition and unfair acts and practices were branded unlawful by the act. Further, it authorized their investigation by the Commission, which would be able to issue "cease and desist" orders against a corporation or, if that failed, to take the corporation to court. The amended act now makes a sweeping declaration that:[22]

[U]nfair methods of competition in or affecting commerce, and unfair and deceptive acts or practices in or affecting commerce, are declared unlawful.

Because it does not deal so directly with problems of monopoly, this act may not appear to be an antitrust law. Since it was amended in 1938 by the Wheeler-Lea Act[23] to stress "deceptive acts or practices," it generally has been concerned with problems of imperfect information like deceptive advertising, rather than of monopoly. But any violation of the Sherman Act also violates the FTC Act and can lead to FTC action. Also, efforts by the FTC in enforcing fair competition have been related to the Clayton and Sherman Acts, so it would be wrong to omit it from the set of antitrust laws.

The Federal Trade Commission was an administrative agency like the Interstate Commerce Commission, intended to allow technical expertise to be brought to bear on social problems. But in its early days it seemed to be formulating codes and trade practices as if in league with businessmen. The Federal Trade Commission Act brought no quick revision in business practice, and America entered the depression decade of the 1930s with most of the sales in many industries concentrated in a few powerful corporations almost as if no effort had been made to control them.

EVENTS AFTER 1914

Soon after passage of the new antitrust legislation in 1914 the nation was engulfed in war; financial and industrial segments of the private economy were engaged to support it. The graduated income tax had been introduced in 1913 to replace revenue lost by tariff reductions that year, and the income tax helped to finance the war effort. Centralization was fostered through the War Industries Board, which finally was given sweeping powers to mobilize the nation's resources for war. Many other governmental agencies were formed. All trust-busting efforts ceased during this period.

At war's end the main concern of government and business alike was to return the economy to private ownership and operation, an aim pushed consistently by the Republicans Warren Harding and Herbert Hoover who held the presidency from 1920 to 1932. The Esch-Cummins Transportation Act of 1920 now sought consolidations of railroads and charged the Interstate Commerce Commission to control rates so a fair return would go to stockholders and fair rates would govern freight and passenger traffic. The act was not entirely successful, in part because the railroads were falling into hard times. Buses, private cars, and trucks, traveling on roads built at public expense, had become common. Then in 1929, after a spectacular spurt of economic growth, came the great crash.

The precarious nature of the economy in the 1930s led to a further postponement of antitrust efforts. Attention was focused instead on legislation and reform that would promote economic recovery and prevent a repetition of the financial collapse of 1929. It is even fair to say that the curative and preventive measures adopted during this period showed no great faith in market competition and some efforts actually promoted monopoly. Adopted for a mixture of purposes, the National Industrial Recovery Act was used in 1933 to support business consolidations in the hope of reviving the economy [5]. After these steps proved unsuccessful, the act was ruled unconstitutional by the Supreme Court. The Miller-Tydings Act of 1937[24] actually exempted manufacturers and retailers from prosecution under Section 1 of the Sherman Act when they participated in certain agreements to adhere to minimum prices, where state laws allowed them to do so. Passage in 1936 of the Robinson-Patman Act, to rewrite the Clayton Act provisions against price discrimination, was the only seemingly antitrust action adopted during the period.

These latter two acts, Miller-Tydings and Robinson-Patman, were passed largely because shopkeepers were numerous and influential; they had political power in their numbers and were able to use it for their own benefit. Of course their arguments were heard also by politicians who were grasping for ways to stimulate the flagging economy. The resale price maintenance scheme allowed under Miller-Tydings helped retailers avoid price competition. Revised sanctions against price discrimination under Robinson-Patman also helped small retailers combat a supermarket revolution that was just beginning by making it more difficult for vendors to give supermarkets favored price treatment on their larger purchases.

Developments in the control exercised by owners—the many shareholders—of corporations were observed for the first time in the 1930s [1]. Dominant ownership by one person or family, which was common in the 1800s, gradually had given way to more widely dispersed ownership as corporations came to have thousands of shareholders. Concern now shifted from robber barons to a phenomenon called *managerial control* in which owners no longer seemed to have tight control over hired managers, who could play one of many owners against another. The pricing behavior of large enterprises also was much criticized because price did not seem to fall with demand in many industries as competitive theory would say it should. This contrary pattern of pricing, called *administered pricing*, was to be much discussed but never convincingly proven to be in widespread use.

Most of the 1940s saw the nation again preoccupied with war. Antimerger provisions of the Clayton Act were made effective after World War II by the Celler-Kefauver Act. Although the concentration of industry was then a topic of some interest, this act was not prompted by great new public concern. The need for it, if the Clayton Act aim ever was to be effective against mergers, had been obvious for a long time but this was one of the first opportunities Congress had to correct it. The Celler-Kefauver Act was also intended to control mergers other than those between competing firms that had been anticipated in the Clayton Act.

Within the government it was thought that moving against mergers with the aid of the Celler-Kefauver Act would at least slow further concentration in industries, which antitrust laws and administrative court decisions had not yet been able to control. The revised Section 7 of the Clayton Act virtually eliminated *horizontal* mergers, mergers between competing firms, and it seriously reduced mergers among firms with *vertical* relationships (that is, mergers between the buyers of a particular input and the suppliers of that input). But there then grew another kind of merger in the 1960s, called a *conglomerate* merger, among firms that had no very obvious business relationship. This form of merger did not have to raise the level of control by one firm over any single line of commerce, but it seemed to harbor anticompetitive possibilities nonetheless, and it brought consternation to those responsible for enforcing antimerger sanctions.

The Antitrust Division of the Justice Department attempted to prevent mergers on various grounds, and there is no doubt the effort prevented a number of them. But enforcement was not consistent and businessmen found it hard to judge when a particular merger would be considered illegal. In 1968 the Justice Department published guidelines indicating the types of mergers they would oppose: horizontal mergers giving the merged firms 10 percent of the industry's sales, vertical mergers where a supplier had 10 percent of a market and a buyer made 6 percent of all purchases, conglomerate mergers involving one firm that might otherwise have entered the other firm's market or if reciprocal buying (a practice where a firm pressures its suppliers to buy their supplies from one of its subsidiary firms) or other practices would lessen competition after the merger. This merger issue recently has constituted a frontier in the antitrust wars, and it continues to draw attention today.

Antitrust policy was given considerable attention in the 1970s, and several small but potentially important changes were made in the laws. In 1974 the maximum fine for antitrust violations was raised to $1 million for corporations and $100,000 for individuals, and the maximum prison sentence was raised from one year to three.[25] In 1975 the Magnuson-Moss FTC Improvements Act[26] expanded the powers of the FTC. Whereas before the FTC was concerned about matters "in" interstate commerce, this act extended its concern to anything "in or affecting" interstate commerce. It allowed the FTC to seek more remedies than before, when the cease and desist order was its only remedy. And the law also strengthened the power of the FTC to promulgate rules for regulating trade.

In 1976 Congress passed the Hart-Scott-Rodino Antitrust Improvements Act[27], which included the *parens patriae* (parent of the state) provision already noted, under which a state attorney general can bring a civil action on behalf of the residents of his state who may have been damaged by an antitrust violation and, if the violation is established, can collect treble damages for the state. In addition, large corporations were required to notify the government before merging, to give more opportunity for opposing the merger.

Today there remain formal exemptions from antitrust law that should be noted. Of course the Clayton Act specifically excluded labor unions. Since 1922 professional baseball has been exempted as a part of sport and not commerce, although curiously this exemption has not been extended to football or other games. Public utilities are exempted where they follow instructions from their states or other regulatory authorities; but they are held accountable to antitrust law when they act in competitive industries. Roughly the same boundary line holds for banking and insurance industries. Quite a wide range of private agricultural and fish marketing agreements would violate antitrust law if they were not specifically allowed under several acts of Congress. Congress also has exempted transportation and allowed agreements among exporters that otherwise would violate antitrust law.

SUMMARY

As the nineteenth century closed the private corporation seemed uncontrolled in the United States, with consolidation of businesses and exploitation of resources both moving at a terrifying pace. When state efforts at control proved unsuccessful, Congress passed the Sherman Act, not as a very clear instruction that civil servants could execute but as a broad aim for courts to take in settling disputes. The Act made monopolizing and restraining trade *crimes*, and also planted incentives for private damage suits against violators of the law. For the Sherman Act to be absorbed by the courts took time, though, and it was not until the turn of the century that it began to block trusts and combinations. Amid swelling public concern, Theodore Roosevelt added vigor to enforcement of the Sherman Act and put in place new institutions like the Department of Commerce to study industry problems. But after some progress the Supreme Court interpreted the Sherman Act so not *every* monopoly or restraint of trade was illegal, only the "unreasonable" ones.

Largely in response to this "rule of reason" evaluation of unreasonable conduct, which was not called for in the Sherman Act, Congress adopted the Clayton Act and the Federal Trade Commission Act. These acts specified unreasonable behavior and created new means for enforcement. They were modified later, mainly to remedy flaws, and there has been no major legislation beyond that. The nation has moved through war, depression, and long periods of international tension since 1914, with public concern seldom focused for long on antitrust policy. So antitrust policy today remains essentially a late Victorian institution, based on the 1890 Sherman Act which was modified by more legislation early in this century but, except for refinements, not altered in a fundamental ways since then.

We have examined here just enough examples of enforcement effort to see how legislation was motivated. Now let us look at enforcement in more detail to see how the laws have been applied.

REFERENCES

1. Adolph A. Berle and Gardiner C. Means. *The Modern Corporation and Private Property*, rev. ed. New York: Harcourt, Brace and World, 1968 (1932).

2. Robert H. Bork. "Legislative Intent and the Policy of the Sherman Act." *Journal of Law and Economics* 9:7-48 (October 1966).

3. Joseph S. Davis. *Essays in the Earlier History of American Corporations*. Cambridge, Mass., Harvard University Press, 1917.

4. Kenneth G. Elzinga and William Breit. *The Antitrust Penalties*. New Haven, Conn.: Yale University Press, 1976.

5. Ellis W. Hawley. *The New Deal and the Problem of Monopoly*. Princeton, N. J.: Princeton University Press, 1966.

6. Robert L. Heilbroner. *The Making of Economic Society*. Englewood Cliffs, N. J.: Prentice-Hall, 1962.

7. Robert L. Heilbroner. *The Economic Transformation of America*. New York: Harcourt Brace Jovanovich, Inc., 1977.

8. J. E. Christopher Hill. *The Century of Revolution 1603-1714*. Edinburgh: Thomas Nelson and Sons, 1961.

9. Richard Hofstadter. *The Age of Reform*. New York: Alfred A. Knopf, 1955.

10. John Jewkes, et al. *The Sources of Invention*. New York: St. Martin, 1969.

11. Matthew Josephson. *The Robber Barons*. New York: Harcourt, Brace and World, 1934.

12. Gabriel Kolko. *Railroads and Regulation, 1877-1916*. Princeton, N. J.: Princeton University Press, 1965.

13. William Letwin. *Law and Economic Policy in America*. New York: Random House, 1965.

14. Albro Martin. "The Troubled Subject of Railroad Regulation in the Gilded Age—A Reappraisal." *The Journal of American History* 61: 339-71 (September 1974).

15. Barrington Moore, Jr. *Social Origins of Dictatorship and Democracy*. Boston: Beacon Press, 1966.

16. Samuel Eliot Morison, Henry Steele Commager, and William E. Leuchtenburg. *The Growth of the American Republic*. London: Oxford University Press, 1969.

17. Ross M. Robertson. *History of the American Economy*. New York: Harcourt, Brace, 1955.

18. Henry R. Seager and Charles A. Gulick, Jr. *Trust and Corporation Problems*. New York: Harper and Brothers, 1929.

19. Hans B. Thorelli. *The Federal Antitrust Policy*. Baltimore: Johns Hopkins University Press, 1955.

END NOTES

1. A description of common law background is available in [19]. See also the historical development in [2], [6], [13] and [15].

2. *Darcy* v. *Allen*, 11 Coke 84, 77 Eng. Rep. 1260 (K. B. 1603). Darcy was Queen Elizabeth's Groom and Allen was the importer of playing cards.

3. For a description of this period see [8].

4. See [3], [7], [16], or [17].

5. For a detailed description of this and other exploits of the period see [11].

6. For pro and con arguments see [12] and [14].

7. For analyses of the passage of the act see [2], [4], [13] and [19].

8. Sherman Act, 15 U. S. C. Sec. 1 (Supp. V 1975).

9. *U. S.* v. *Employing Plasterers Association of Chicago*, 347 U. S. 186 (1954).

10. Sherman Act, 15 U. S. C. Sec. 2 (Supp. V 1975).

11. See the Hart-Scott-Rodino Antitrust Improvements Act of 1976, 15 U. S. C. A. Sec. 15c (1977).

12. *U. S.* v. *E. C. Knight Co.*, 156 U. S. 1(1895).

13. *U. S.* v. *Trans-Missouri Freight Assn.*, 166 U. S. 290 (1897).

14. *U. S.* v. *Addyston Pipe and Steel Co.*, 85 Fed. 271 (1898) and 175 U. S. 211 (1899).

15. The attorney general was Philander C. Knox, a successful corporation lawyer before being appointed by President McKinley.

16. *Northern Securities Co.* v. *U. S.*, 193 U. S. 197 (1904).

17. *Standard Oil Co. of N. J.* v. *U. S.*, 221 U. S. 1(1911).

18. For description of the reform period see [9].

19. Robinson-Patman Act, 15 U. S. C. Sec. 13 (1970).

20. Clayton Act Sec. 3, 15 U. S. C. Sec 14 (1970).

21. Clayton Act Sec. 7, 15 U. S. C. Sec. 18 (1970).

22. Federal Trade Commission Act, 15 U. S. C. Sec. 45 (Supp. V 1975).

23. Wheeler-Lea Act, 15 U. S. C. Sec. 45 (1970).

24. Miller-Tydings Act, 15 U. S. C. Sec. 1 (1970).

25. Antitrust Procedures and Penalties Act, 15 U. S. C. Sec. 16 (Supp. V 1975).

26. Magnuson-Moss FTC Improvements Act of 1975, 15 U. S. C. A. Sec. 45 (1977).

27. Hart-Scott-Rodino Antitrust Improvements Act of 1976, 15 U. S. C. A. Sec. 15c (1977).

Antitrust *4*
Enforcement

The effect of legislation, particularly legislation like the original Sherman Act that leaves wide scope for court interpretation, depends on how it is enforced. With respect to antitrust, the Antitrust Division of the Justice Department and the Federal Trade Commission have played crucial enforcement roles. In addition, there are private suits seeking treble damages, now augmented because state attorneys general can sue to recover damages suffered by their states' residents. Also of importance are the penalties that can be imposed for violating antitrust laws.

We shall begin by describing enforcement agencies and procedures plus available remedies for violations. The we shall turn to examine actual enforcement efforts in four important areas: monopolization, restraint of trade, merger, and unfair and deceptive practice. Monopolization is obviously important but cases against it have been handicapped by lack of a clear definition for monopoly and inconsistent interpretation of what is undesirable about it. Sanctions against merger have been enforced more effectively in recent years but here too a clear understanding of consequences of some mergers is still missing. Restraints of trade are some of the best defined offenses, while unfair and deceptive practices are still being elaborated.

LEGAL PROCEDURES AND ENFORCEMENT AGENCIES

The court case is the best known legal procedure. One party files a complaint (the *plaintiff*) against another party who becomes the defendant (the *respondent*). The parties make extensive preparations before a trial begins with court rulings governing such matters as the information each party is entitled to obtain from the other under what are called *discovery* procedures. The trial typically will take place in one of our ninety Federal District Courts and will be filled with arguments about both fact and law. Criminal defendants always can insist on a jury trial, and a party in a treble damage action may also request trial by jury. Because specialized knowledge is so important in antitrust cases, a jury typically will receive extensive instructions from the judge about what issues it is to treat and what the law requires in deciding them.

Once the trial ends either party may appeal the decision to the next higher level of federal court, the Appeals Court for its region (there are eleven), but the appeal can only concern points of law. Eventually the case may even be appealed to the third and final level, the Supreme Court, and heard there if four of the nine members of the Court find the point of law in the appeal sufficiently important to warrant attention.[1] With time for appeals, an antitrust case may take five years or even longer. The way a point of law is finally settled will be binding in future cases under the *stare decisis* principle discussed in Chapter 1.

Provision was made in the Sherman Act for the Department of Justice to initiate both civil and criminal actions. The Department of Justice can also take a defendant to court under the Clayton Act but, since its violations are not regarded as criminal acts, it prompts only civil suits. As we have noted, treble-damage provisions in the Sherman Act and the Clayton Act create an incentive for private parties to bring actions themselves, thereby enlarging the enforcement effort, and state attorneys general can sue on their citizens' behalf. The Federal Trade Commission was created to compel compliance through administrative procedures. Its main weapon has been an order to *cease and desist* from using objectionable practices; since 1975 it has been able to go to court and seek other remedies.[2]

Criminal and civil actions differ in that criminal actions are to *punish* wrongdoing, whereas civil actions have the object of *preventing violations* of the law in the future and *compensating* for damages suffered. In bringing a criminal proceeding under the Sherman Act, the Justice Department must first seek a grand jury indictment. Grand juries can only be used for criminal cases; they allow a thorough investigation prior to trial because grand juries have sweeping powers. Sometimes both criminal and civil actions are undertaken against the same violation so one remedy may be inflicted even though others fail. Indeed, a civil action may be undertaken even where a criminal action already has been decided against the Justice Department, because the standard of proof for a civil wrong is not as high and so the department still might win the civil case.

The outcome of a civil action is not limited to an award of damages or to an order that some objectionable conduct be stopped. In order to prevent future violations the Department of Justice may obtain an injunction limiting the behavior of the offending firm in many other ways or requiring reports to the Justice Department and subjecting the firm to special government oversight for a specified future time. A court decision in a civil case may even call for dissolution of a firm. *Consent decrees* sometimes result from civil proceedings; they are judicial orders that can be altered or interpreted only by a court and from which violations are punished by contempt. Consent decrees arise out of agreement by government and defendant before a case is decided at trial and often before any evidence is introduced in a case. They do not have the force of precedent and leave behind no extensive record. They often are practical compromises, sometimes saving a firm the bother of a case and the embarrassment of confessing error and liability, or saving the government from prosecuting what it has come to see as a weak case.

The Federal Trade Commission (FTC) is not a court; it is an administrative agency like the Interstate Commerce Commission (ICC) and its procedures are less formal than those of a court. In appointing its five members to their seven-year terms, the president must choose persons from more than one political party; they must also be confirmed by the Senate. These steps are to make the Commission more expertly specialized, and less political, than the executive branch's attorney general. Usually a complaint from industry or from someone in government will start an investigation but the FTC also initiates studies on its own, not only through its staff in Washington but also using the resources of its regional offices.

A complaint is adjudicated through an FTC hearing, overseen by an administrative law judge. At the close of the hearing the Commission issues a decision that can be quite broad in scope, often going beyond the particular action complained of to forbid the firm to accomplish its aim by other means as well. In certain circumstances *consumer redress* actions may be instituted in the courts if the Commission finds that a refund or payment of damages is in order. It also can issue cease and desist orders to prevent unlawful action in the future. FTC decisions are subject to review in federal courts of appeal. If appeal is not pursued, the FTC order is final. Each violation of such an order, and a separate violation can occur every day that the order is disobeyed, can incur a fine of up to $10,000.

The overlapping jurisdiction of the Department of Justice and the FTC—they share enforcement responsibility for the Clayton Act and their jurisdictions can overlap in other areas as well—could lead to difficulties. Each agency is careful to inform the other of its proposed investigations before it proceeds with them, though, so efforts can be coordinated effectively where that is needed. Although a clearer division of duties has been urged [6], and might simplify governmental enforcement efforts, problems of conflict and lack of coordination do not appear to have been debilitating [1,

p. 33]. It is even possible that, as in the private economy, the competition of two government agencies can be a good thing.

REMEDIES

In Congress, both before and after passage of the Sherman Act, many possible remedies for violations were debated.[3] There were proposals to withhold federal services from antitrust violators, such as access to federal courts or even mail service, or limit the transportation of their goods in interstate commerce, or even to make them forfeit their property. A reduction in tariff protection was actively urged for industries guilty of antitrust violations, while taxes also were suggested, particularly for industries unaffected by tariffs. Simple publicity was recommended based mainly on systematic government inspection of a company's records although rewards to informers were also suggested. But none of these remedies was adopted.

Five main remedies exist today for violations of the antitrust laws. First, a private party who feels injured by an antitrust violation may sue, and on winning may not only prevent the harmful action from continuing but also collect from the antitrust violator three times the amount of damages suffered (plus court costs including a reasonable attorney's fee). As we have noted, states can now bring this essentially private action on behalf of their residents under the *parens patriae* provision of the Antitrust Improvements Act of 1976. Under the Clayton Act a private party may sue to prevent future injury, too. Four remedies can result from public action: fines, jail terms for individuals, injunctions, and structural changes to the firm that could require the sale or other disposition of some of its assets.

Whether to allow compensation for single, double, or treble the amount of damages suffered due to antitrust violations was debated in Congress, but three-fold damages, from the English Statute of Monopolies, was finally adopted for the Sherman Act. Although the treble-damage provision gives incentive for private enforcement of the law it has not been entirely successful as a remedy. To recover damages, a private party has to show harm by some action forbidden under the antitrust laws, and proof of damages can be difficult. When a buyer is damaged by an excessively high price it is not so hard to prove, because the difference between that price and an estimated competitive price can be multiplied by the actual quantity bought for a reasonable estimate. But if an illegal practice prevents someone from entering a line of business, that person will have no records to show what might have been earned; proof of the loss suffered will then be difficult to show. The treble-damage provision also invites nuisance actions that merely harass competitors. Whereas fines have statutory upper limits, treble-damage payments have no upper limit beyond the need to prove injury. The damage payments are tax deductible, however.

By amendments to the Sherman Act in 1974, a guilty individual in a criminal case may be fined up to $100,000 and a guilty corporation up to $1,000,000 for each violation of a section of the Sherman Act.[4] The effect of the fines can be magnified, too, because corporate *fines are not deductible from corporate income for tax purposes*; furthermore, where individuals are fined, their reimbursement by the corporation often is not allowed. A record of fines levied under antitrust laws since 1890 compiled by Richard Posner [5] shows that, in those criminal cases where fines were imposed, the average fine per case did not reach $100,000 until the 1960s. For the large corporations involved, that would be only a tiny fraction of sales or profit.

An individual can be sent to prison for three years for violating the Sherman Act, which has been considered a felony since 1974. A compilation by Kenneth G. Elzinga and William Breit [3, pp. 34-37] shows jail sentences to be growing more common after they were used for the electrical equipment conspiracy in the early 1960s. But, of ninety defendants subject to criminal sanction from 1966 through 1973, when the crime was a misdemeanor with a maximum sentence of one year, only twenty-five served time in jail, the longest stretch being nine months.

An injunction may forbid a certain action without imposing any penalty for its having been carried on in the past. Indeed, the injunction may involve no real penalty, although most injunctions do prohibit an antitrust defendant from some specified future business conduct. When the injunction constrains a firm from actions, essentially forever, it can impose a cost or limitation amounting to a significant penalty. For example, Swift and Company has not been allowed certain merger actions under terms of a 1903 injunction;[5] that limitation has almost certainly constrained the company from operating as it would have wished.

Structural relief is the most dramatic weapon in the antitrust arsenal because it involves changes in the size and shape of the business unit itself. Appropriate structural relief is seldom easy to devise, however, and is usually hard to accomplish. Deciding what part of the firm to divest is especially difficult when the firm involved is very large. A district court judge cannot be expected to know all the consequences of such an action. Accomplishing divestiture is also difficult because inevitable delays can thwart the intended purpose; by the time a divestiture decree is carried out, that portion of a firm to be divested may have been stripped of its strategic value. Kenneth G. Elzinga [2] studied thirty-nine cases involving such decrees under the Celler-Kefauver Act and found three-fourths of them seriously deficient or unsuccessful.

We are thus left with no penalty that has shown a clear record of unambiguous success in deterring anticompetitive action. By turning now to enforcement efforts we may see whether this failure is due to the nature of the law, the penalties, or the way the penalties have been employed.

ENFORCEMENT ACTION

Briefly for review, recall that the antitrust laws make it illegal:

(1) To monopolize, to attempt to monopolize, or to combine or conspire to monopolize trade (Sherman Act, Section 2)

(2) To enter a contract, combination, or conspiracy in restraint of trade (Sherman Act, Section 1) like collusion among existing sellers, exclusion of other sellers (also Clayton Act, Section 3), or discrimination (Clayton Act, Section 2 as amended by Robinson-Patman Act)

(3) To merge if the effect may substantially lessen competition or tend to create a monopoly (Clayton Act, Section 7 as amended by Celler-Kefauver Act)

(4) To use unfair or deceptive practices (Federal Trade Commission Act, Section 5 as amended)

Having described the agencies charged with antitrust enforcement and sketched the available penalties, we now shall examine enforcement efforts in the four broad areas just summarized: monopolization, restraint or trade, merger, and unfair or deceptive practice.[7]

Monopolization

A question that arose early from Section 2 of the Sherman Act was whether antitrust effort should oppose monopoly *power* or monopoly *conduct*. The law did not exactly oppose the existence of monopoly, it opposed *monopolizing* (the law, remember, made it unlawful "to monopolize, attempt to monopolize, or combine or conspire with others to monopolize trade"). When the Supreme Court held that Standard Oil Company was an illegal monopoly in 1911, it emphasized the unreasonableness of the company's conduct as the basis for its judgment rather than the fact that the firm possessed monopoly power. As we noted earlier, this attention to the reasonableness of a monopoly's conduct in deciding Section 2 Sherman Act cases is known as the rule of reason.

After the *Standard Oil* decision the rule of reason came to be relied on often. In the same year as the Standard Oil decision the American Tobacco Company was found to have acted illegally, largely because of unreasonable conduct, and was dissolved into fourteen separate companies.[8] These decisions rejected the narrow scope for antitrust in the *E. C. Knight* case,[9] which allowed the E. C. Knight Trust on the ground that it was a manufacturer not in interstate commerce even though it controlled 95 percent of the nation's sugar market. But, while the decisions in 1911 broadened the Court's view of the scope of the act to include manufacturing, in establishing the rule of reason it also narrowed the ground for judging monopoly on its conduct rather than its power alone.

The rule of reason did not have to affect crucially the outcome of either the Standard Oil case or the American Tobacco case because monopolization in those cases was easy to see; the reasonableness judgment served more to clinch the Court's findings of guilt. But starting in 1916 the possibility of that rule undercutting antitrust efforts became clear. The American Can Company had controlled 90 percent of the production of tin cans yet was not convicted of violating the Sherman Act because it "had done nothing of which any competitor or consumer of cans complains, or anything which strikes a disinterested outsider as unfair or unethical."[10] In the court's view it had not been unreasonable in its conduct.

There followed in 1920 an even more remarkable four-to-three Court decision finding the United States Steel Corporation not in violation of the law. The corporation had been built from 180-odd companies. It controlled two thirds of the industry in 1901, when it was also fixing prices. But the court deemed its monopoly attempt unsuccessful and judged its price-fixing ineffective because by 1920 its meetings with rival steel producers had been abandoned. The corporation still controlled half the industry in 1920 but the court said "the law does not make mere size an offense."[11] This U. S. Steel decision forced the Justice Department into a more modest view of antitrust violations.

The passage of the Clayton and Federal Trade Commission Acts in 1914 did not halt the rule of reason because courts could see these two laws as legitimizing attention to business firm conduct rather than monopoly power itself. So during the boom following World War I, into the Great Crash, and through the 1930s, antitrust effort against monopoly languished. It was revived when Thurman Arnold became the aggressive head of the Antitrust Division in 1938. But even the thorough cases his organization developed might have accomplished little without a profound decision in 1945 against the rule of reason, written by a respected judge in the Second Circuit in New York, Learned Hand.

The Aluminum Company (Alcoa) case fell to Learned Hand's court under unusual circumstances. From 1903 Alcoa essentially had controlled aluminum production, at first because it held crucial patents. In 1937 the government charged that Alcoa had monopolized the manufacture of virgin aluminum, plus the sale of aluminum products, and maintained its monopoly through unfair practices such as "spotting plants"—discouraging new entrants by building plants in areas before demand was great enough to sustain them—or ruining fabricators by squeezing the price spread between finished goods and raw aluminum. Dissolution was asked as the remedy. When a trial court found Alcoa not guilty the government immediately appealed. But because they had participated in earlier litigation in the case, four justices of the Supreme Court disqualified themselves from hearing the appeal, leaving the Supreme Court without a quorum of six. Congress then amended the judicial code so an Appeals Court could serve as court of last resort in this peculiar circumstance, and that is how the case came before a panel headed by Judge Hand.

The approach taken by Judge Hand was to see first whether monopoly power existed; for this question he focused on defining the market. Alcoa manufactured more than 90 percent of virgin aluminum ingot consumed in the United States (the rest was imported); if scrap was included as part of the market the company still accounted for more than 60 percent. If scrap was included and Alcoa's consumption of its own ingots was excluded, as the company argued it should be, its share would fall to a third of the market. Judge Hand thought 90 percent of a market would constitute monopoly, but 60 percent was doubtful and 33 percent was not monopoly. He concluded that because aluminum scrap was the result of earlier Alcoa virgin ingot production, the virgin ingot market was the crucial one, and, in view of its 90 percent control there, he accepted the government's position that Alcoa had a monopoly in aluminum. He then had to deal with the company's claim that even if monopoly power existed it had not been unreasonably exercised.

On this question Learned Hand boldly took a compelling position against the rule of reason. The distinction between monopoly power and its exercise he regarded as "purely formal; it would be valid only so long as the monopoly remained wholly inert; it would disappear as soon as the monopoly began to operate; for, when it did—that is, as soon as it began to sell at all—it must sell at some price and the only price at which it could sell is a price which it itself fixed. Thereafter the power and its exercise must needs coalesce." [12] To bolster his position that the possession of market power was the sole test of monopoly he pointed out how absurd it would be to hold per se unlawful a collusive agreement among several firms in a market (as the Sherman Act did) when, if the same firms all merged into one and behaved "reasonably" there would be no violation of law. As he saw it, Congress "did not condone 'good trusts' and condemn 'bad' ones; it forbade all."

The decision about a remedy in this case was postponed until aluminum plants built during World War II and owned by the government were disposed of. But when relief did come, at the hands of Judge Knox in Chicago in 1950,[13] it was modest. Alcoa had to license patents and sever its connection with Aluminum Ltd. of Canada, while the government's wartime aluminum plants went to the Kaiser and Reynolds companies which, with Alcoa, came to share the market for aluminum. However, a redefinition of monopoly had been achieved by Judge Hand, for in a 1946 case of conspiracy against the three leading cigarette producers[14] collusion was inferred for the first time from evidence of identical buying and selling prices; no special intent was said to be needed as long as monopoly resulted.

An interesting elaboration of this revived Section 2 of the Sherman Act came from Judge Charles Wyzanski in his United Shoe Machinery Corporation decision in 1953.[15] He argued that when monopoly power was due substantially to barriers caused by its own practices and not due entirely to other factors, even though the practices were not predatory or otherwise counter to Section 1 of the Sherman Act, the monopoly would be unlawful under Section 2. He effectively imposed a higher standard of behavior on monopolies. Where the company produced 90 percent of U. S. shoe machinery he found its practices of only leasing machines and not selling them, of using certain exclusive long-term contracts, and of possible price discrimination, while not necessarily illegal for a firm in a less secure market position, were enough to allow United Shoe Machinery to exclude competitors and so were illegal.[16]

With the exception of some current government cases and a recent increase in private damage suits, little antitrust activity has been carried out against monopoly since 1953. During that period much effort was directed instead at preventing oligopoly and monopoly by moving to stop mergers. Before examining this effort against mergers, let us consider restraint of trade to see how problems in treating oligopolistic collusion encouraged the antimerger effort.

Restraint of Trade

In addition to the problem of monopoly itself there are several unlawful practices that can restrain trade and tend toward the same result as monopoly. We shall discuss three: (1) *collusion* of parties in a market, which allows them to act together to profit much as a monopolist would alone; (2) *exclusion* of parties from a market, which also brings partial monopoly benefits to those already in the market; and (3) *price discrimination*, a manifestation of monopoly power that can be economically inefficient and usually is inequitable. These practices can violate Section 1 of the Sherman Act, or the Clayton Act.

Collusion involves some sort of agreement among firms. Examples would be the eighteen railroads in the *Trans-Missouri* case that fixed prices for freight haulage and the six producers of cast iron pipe in the *Addyston* case that divided markets and participated in a combination to fix prices, both found per se illegal without any showing of consequences or reasonableness needed. The per se illegality of price-fixing no doubt contributes to the notable enforcement success enjoyed by the government against it. Except for a contradictory judgment in the depression conditions of 1933,[17] the Supreme Court has maintained uniformly a position that Section 1 of the Sherman Act is to protect consumers by forbidding price-fixing and the rigging of markets. Any agreement to fix prices is to be condemned however reasonable the result appears.

Of course conspirators might still escape punishment if they can successfully keep their price-fixing secret. The most celebrated antitrust case in recent years probably was the electrical equipment price conspiracy of 1961,[18] in which representatives of twenty-nine companies communicated secretly, sometimes in coded messages, and arranged clandestine meetings at hotels under assumed names. As bidders on large contracts for heavy electrical generators, transformers, and switchgear, they agreed among themselves who would offer the lowest price. Their mechanisms for choosing who would be low bidder ranged from a simple alphabetical rotation among themselves to random selection, like picking the name out of a hat, and even to a complicated system based on phases of the moon. The agreed-upon low bidder would inform others of his bid, and they would then submit higher ones. Some contracts had to be shared, however, in order that the amount of work could be allocated to the conspirators' mutual satisfaction. This led to their undoing, for when bids from several firms on government projects were identical—to many decimal places—the buyer understandably grew suspicious.

An even more difficult problem arises when there are only a few firms in a market, the market situation that is called *oligopoly*. Being few in number, oligopolists can see the effects their actions have on one another. They can cooperate tacitly without ever sending any message, except the message implicit in their own actions. Because business behavior of this sort manifests no coded messages or meetings in hotel rooms, no party need confess to a single self-evident misdeed. Separate firms simply act in a cooperative way as they pursue their own best interests. Although their behavior may not look very competitive, it is hard for a court to rule that it is illegal.

The Supreme Court had been willing to find implied conspiracy, however, as early as 1914. In that year a lumber dealers' trade association was prevented from circulating among its members the names of wholesalers who were selling directly to consumers because evidence that dealers would refuse to do business with these offending wholesalers was taken to reveal a conspiracy.[19] A conspiracy was again inferred in an important 1939 case from the signing by eight film distributors of similar contracts with a theater chain operator.[20] Among other things, the contracts fixed admission charges. Each signer knew the others were signing the contracts, and that was accepted by the Court as evidence of conspiracy under the Sherman Act.

The inferential conspiracy case was taken farthest against the Big Three cigarette manufacturers, American Tobacco, Liggett and Myers, and R. J. Reynolds, along with associated companies and individuals in a suit finally settled in 1946.[21] There was no evidence of meetings or illegal communications, yet concerted action by defendants was alleged to have prevented effective competition. Although the evidence of market power was circumstantial, by drawing on *Northern Securities* and Judge Hand's *Alcoa* decision it was argued successfully by the government that possession of power was all that had to be shown, not that it was exercised or that any specific harm to a competitor or other party needed to be established.

After agreement by competitors to identical contract provisions, identical patent licensing provisions, and other identical policies was found illegal, this tacit collusion argument faltered and the antimonopoly surge begun by Thurman Arnold faltered too. The Court rejected parallel action alone as proof of conspiracy in several 1953 and 1954 decisions,[22] and the Antitrust Division and the FTC turned their attention to mergers and other matters. Even during the period when tacit collusion had been more easily found by the Court, the remedies—usually denial of certain practices—had not been particularly painful to firms. The problem of sympathetic action by oligopolistic firms remains almost untouched by antitrust policy even today.

Exclusion reduces the access potential sellers have to a market, thereby benefiting the sellers who are already there. It can support a collusive price-fixing arrangement by preventing goods from noncolluding suppliers to reach consumers at a lower price. One of the most obvious means of excluding competitors is by a contract that gives one party an exclusive right, say to sell a product in a defined geographic area. The exclusive right is especially likely in the case of a product sufficiently complex and important to require explanation for effective sale and good maintenance service for effective use. In such cases manufacturers want to avoid cut-throat competition on price alone because it might prevent adequate explanation to customers of the product's operating features or an appreciation of its durability. At least that is the type of argument used by producers to justify the assignment of exclusive selling rights for automobiles, bicycles, mens' suits, and other products in certain well-defined territories. But the Court has required that the dealers be free to seek and accept customers from each others' territories, especially if they take legal title to the product they retail and if its manufacturer is a leading one.[23] Otherwise exclusive territorial divisions have been treated as per se violations of Section 1 of the Sherman Act.

A related issue is whether the dealer can be restricted by a producer to carrying that producer's line of products exclusively. Such a limitation can approach what is called a *total requirements contract*, and agreement by a buyer to accept all he might need of a certain line of product from a single seller, which is forbidden by Section 3 of the Clayton Act. Producers who used any such contracts were repeatedly enjoined, from the 1920s through the 1940s, as long as they were dominant in their industries.[24] Although since the 1950s the FTC has required that actual injury be likely from such contracts, and the Supreme Court also has required a showing of significant effect,[25] the practice today is almost illegal per se.[26]

Tying contracts were also outlawed by Section 3 of the Clayton Act. A tying contract typically requires that a consumer buy a second product in order to obtain the one he wants; the second product is "tied" to the first. Because it gives the seller of one product an advantage in selling the second one, it can serve to exclude others, and that is deemed to be unfair. Tying usually requires a monopoly of the first product, so it can be attacked as evidence of monopoly under Section 2 of the Sherman Act; it is also a restrictive practice under Section 1. Tying has come to be a violation per se when the firm using it has a substantial market share.

Price discrimination was made explicitly unlawful by Section 2 of the Clayton Act. In opposing price discrimination Congress has been concerned less directly with consequences for consumers and rather more with competitors being destroyed, as when a large trust keeps prices low in a particular area for that purpose. When the Robinson-Patman Act was passed in 1936 to amend the Clayton Act, the protection of competitors was made more precise, largely to protect small grocers against the development of supermarket chains. Most cases of price discrimination still arise in channels of distribution for goods, where a range of wholesaling functions is performed. Because different ways of organizing may require different wholesaling services, it is difficult to ensure uniform services or prices. When the distribution channels develop new forms as they change with time, uniformity in pricing arrangements becomes especially difficult to sustain.

Whenever the price charged to one customer for a particular good or service differs from that charged another, price discrimination is suspected. But the good or service may not be identical if there are different customer locations, different associated services provided, or different times of day, week, or year for delivery. Marginal costs for providing the good or service can differ by location, service, or time of production or delivery, so confirming that price discrimination actually has occurred is difficult. Also, price discrimination by a small firm may be judged suitably aggressive competitive behavior and go untouched, whereas the same action by a dominant firm would be opposed.

Generally, brokerage payments have been allowed to go only to independent brokers, not to chains of retailers who claim to be performing a broker's functions. A seller can allow a discount to a buyer who saves him costs by taking over merchandising functions, provided the seller makes the same offer available to all. Quantity discounts also can be allowed when justified by cost savings as long as they are not designed so they benefit only certain buyers. Many discounts for different kinds of dealers—wholesalers or retailers for examples—are accepted as long as members of these different functional categories do not compete.

Merger

Looking back over antitrust enforcement efforts we can see that the early campaign against monopolies formed at the turn of the century lasted until

1920, when the U. S. Steel decision showed how the ground on which monopoly could be attacked had been weakened by the rule of reason. A second effort starting in 1938 eventually weakened the rule of reason. This effort ended in 1953 when parallel business behavior was no longer accepted as conclusive evidence of collusion, thereby placing cooperative oligopolistic behavior seemingly beyond the reach of antitrust. The Celler-Kefauver Act was passed in 1950 to close loopholes in Section 7 of the Clayton Act by defining mergers more thoroughly and to extend control over all types of mergers. So it was natural to try to stop at least the furtherance of oligopolistic market organization, which the government now seemed unable to control, by preventing its achievement through merger. Yet in the 1960s the nation entered what has been described as its third great merger wave.

Mergers are usually classified as *horizontal, vertical,* or *conglomerate,* based on the markets affected. Horizontal mergers involve producers in the same market, such as the merger proposed in the 1950s between two steel producers, Bethlehem Steel Company and Youngstown Sheet and Tube Company. Vertical mergers are between firms that operate in different markets along the path a product takes from raw material to the consumer. Conglomerate mergers are between firms in markets that are unrelated to each other; such mergers are thought to be for diversification. Of these three types, the horizontal merger is the one that is most threatening to competition because it involves the combination of otherwise competing firms.

A thorough examination of complicated market definitions was carried out in the case of a merger between the Brown Shoe Company and the G. R. Kinney Company, decided by the Supreme Court in 1962.[27] The amended Section 7 of the Clayton Act describes the market where it forbids mergers whose effect may be substantially to lessen competition or tend to create a monopoly as "any line of commerce in any section of the country." Both firms manufactured shoes and also sold them at retail, so the case had both horizontal and vertical aspects. The Supreme Court noted from the record in the case that a tendency toward concentration could be seen in the industry; since the Court interpreted the law as intending to prevent a lessening of competition in its incipiency, only a probability of damage to competition was needed as proof without a certainty it would result. After a careful sorting into the lines of commerce of men's, women's and children's shoes, and studying local competitive effects amid a national market, the Court found that even though some economies might have been achieved by the firms through merger it was sufficiently threatening to competition to be denied.

Attention to all the specific features of particular markets in the *Brown Shoe* case seemed to yield to more general guidelines when larger market shares were involved in the *Philadelphia National Bank* case[28] a year later. Here the Philadelphia National Bank and Girard Trust Corn Exchange Bank were the second and third largest in what was judged to be the relevant

market: banking services in the Philadelphia area. From market share cal-
culations in the record of the case the Court concluded that bringing together firms with 22 percent and 15 percent shares of that market would, in the
absence of evidence to the contrary, substantially lessen competition. The
government was successful in virtually all of its early Section 7 cases against
merger. Even a large holding by the DuPont Corporation of General Motors stock was disallowed,[29] without there being an actual merger, on the
ground that DuPont's holdings would give it advantages over other suppliers in winning the automaker's paint, fabric, and other purchases. Courts
have also treated genuine vertical mergers with suspicion, and very few significant ones have occurred since 1950.

The so-called conglomerate merger seems unlikely to create a monopoly
since it involves completely unrelated firms. But when one of the firms is a
prominent potential new entrant to the other's industry their merger has
been disallowed.[30] Or if the merger would lead to a situation where one part
of the new firm could extract from any former supplier some obligation to
purchase its other products in turn, the merger could be turned aside.[31] If
one of the firms involved is among the largest two hundred in the nation, or
if any other anticompetitive effect can be discerned, a merger may also be
prevented. Since passage of the Hart-Scott-Rodino Antitrust Improvements
Act of 1976 large companies planning any kind of merger or acquisition
must notify the Justice Department in advance and wait a specified period
before consummating the planned action. This allows the Justice Department time to decide whether the action might have anticompetitive effects
that would violate antitrust laws. Thus, with respect to mergers, the antitrust effort since the Celler-Kefauver Act has been enforced so that merger
can be used today only sparingly, if at all, by a large firm wanting to grow
larger.

Unfair and Deceptive Practice

Partly as a result of new powers from the Magnuson-Moss FTC Improvements Act, perhaps partly in response to criticism of its past performance,
and partly because of new additions to its resources (from 1970 to 1977 its
budget tripled to $53,000,000), the FTC has been particularly vigorous in its
recent attacks on unfair practices. One example where it has brandished its
new authority to make rules in decisive ways concerns the funeral industry.
So that bereaved next of kin are less apt to be exploited by ruthless funeral
directors, the FTC has issued a rule requiring that directors give prices over
the telephone, display inexpensive caskets along with expensive ones, get
permission before embalming, and itemize costs. Funeral directors bitterly
oppose this rule. Industry representatives used to be able to influence FTC
rule-making by quietly cultivating the rule-makers. But as now interpreted
by the FTC the Magnuson-Moss Act makes all meetings with industry rep-

resentatives public and thus robs industries of what was once substantial be-hind-the-scenes influence.

Even though strictly speaking it is not an unfair or deceptive practice, the FTC has tried to curtail the opportunity conglomerate firms have to conceal information about their separate product lines. Separate corpora-tions whose shares are traded on major stock exchanges must publish annu-al reports to satisfy requirements set by the Securities and Exchange Com-mission (SEC) to insure that investors are informed. However, if the firms merged they might publish only one report.[32] Managers then could lump to-gether successful and unsuccessful activities, perhaps to hide their own mis-takes and surely to keep potential competitors from knowledge of their suc-cesses, so conglomerate firms could save the expense of reporting and keep secrets at the same time. The FTC has proposed *line of business* reporting by all firms to make information by each product line publicly available. Slightly more than half the firms that received line-of-business question-naires from the FTC have filed suit to enjoin the reporting program, howev-er, objecting to the cost of preparing the reports. The FTC can point out that merely ennumerating the reporting cost does not support nondisclosure when the lack of information may be more costly in faulty resource alloca-tion than the cost of the reports. But the dispute continues.

SUMMARY

Two large government agencies, the Antitrust Division of the Justice De-partment and the Federal Trade Commission, pursue enforcement of anti-trust laws. Enforcement effort also comes from private parties and state at-torneys general seeking treble damages from violations. Some of the speci-fic rules of law that have resulted, like the illegality of price-fixing, are un-ambiguous. But many decisions have been difficult to guess in advance and have been inconsistent on important matters, so the record is not a very clear one. The record also is so large that we cannot begin to capture it here, so the businessman who wants to be in compliance with the law will need either a great fund of legal knowledge or a good lawyer, and even then he cannot always be sure.

The five main remedies for violation of antitrust laws have not seemed particularly effective. They are: private suits seeking treble damages, fines up to statutory limits, incarceration of employees responsible for violations, injunctions, and structural changes such as dissolution or divestiture. These remedies leave much scope for discretion in working out solutions, and, be-ing accomplished primarily in different district courts, the remedies have been applied timidly and not very uniformly.

Two major antitrust efforts may be distinguished since the Sherman Act, one from 1904 to 1920 against turn-of-the-century monopolists and another from 1938 to 1953 aimed largely at the restrictive practices of oligopoly firms. An effort against mergers was also undertaken in the 1960s, and important new antitrust cases have recently been undertaken. It is clear from a study of past cases that in each legal decision much effort goes to settling the matter at issue in a sensible way that complies with proper legal procedures. In part because the rule that results from an important case is one deemed equitable in the circumstances, and focused mainly to that end, it may not be the simplest to administer in future. Indeed, the process seems oblivious to how cases arise because rules are numerous and complicated, and delaying tactics can affect greatly their economic effect. We might therefore wonder just how competitive our economy is under the antitrust laws.

REFERENCES

1. Phillip Agreeda. *Antitrust Analysis*. Boston: Little, Brown, 1967.
2. Kenneth G. Elzinga. "The Antimerger Law: Pyrrhic Victories?" *Journal of Law and Economics* 12: 43-78 (April 1969).
3. Kenneth G. Elzinga and William Breit. *The Antitrust Penalties*. New Haven, Conn.: Yale University Press, 1976.
4. A. D. Neale. *The Antitrust Laws of the U. S. A.* 2nd ed. Cambridge: Cambridge University Press, 1970.
5. Richard A. Posner. "A Statistical Study of Antitrust Enforcement." *Journal of Law and Economics* 13: 365-419 (October 1970).
6. George J. Stigler, Chairman. "The Report of the President's Task Force on Productivity and Competition." Washington, D. C.: *Congressional Record— Senate*. June 16, 1969, pp. 56473-56480.
7. Jerrold G. Van Cise. *The Federal Antitrust Laws*. Washington, D. C.: American Enterprise Institute, 1975.
8. Clair Wilcox and William G. Shepherd. *Public Policies Toward Business*. 5th ed. Homewood, Ill.: Richard D. Irwin, Inc., 1975.

END NOTES

1. Under some circumstances, which were made more limiting in 1974, an antitrust case of "general public importance to the administration of justice" can go directly from the District Court to the Supreme Court. See 15 U. S. C. Secs. 28, 29 (Supp. V 1975).
2. FTC *Procedures and Rules of Practice*, 16 C. F. R., Ch. 1A, 3CCH Trade Reg. Rep. para 9801 et seq., (1974), and FTC Improvements Act of 1975, 15 U. S. C. A. Sec. 45 (1977).

3. The following account relies heavily on an excellent recent summary by Kenneth G. Elzinga and William Breit in [3].

4. Sherman Act, 15 U. S. C., Secs. 1, 2 (Supp. V 1975).

5. See *Swift and Company* v. *U. S.* 196 U. S. 375 (1905).

6. The history of antitrust case decisions is reported in many books on antitrust or public policy toward business. For a good example see [8]. For more detailed description of antitrust law and cases see [1] and [4], and for a concise treatment see [7].

7. *Standard Oil Co. of N. J.* v. *U. S.*, 221 U. S. 1(1911).

8. *U. S.* v. *American Tobacco Co.*, 221 U. S. 106 (1911).

9. *U. S.* v. *E. C. Knight Co.*, 156 U. S. 1 (1895).

10. *U. S.* v. *American Can Co.*, 230 F. 859, 861 (1916).

11. *U. S.* v. *United States Steel Corp.*, 251 U. S. 417, 451 (1920).

12. *U. S.* v. *Aluminum Co. of America*, 148 F. 2nd 416, 428 (1945).

13. 91 F. Supp. 333 (1950).

14. *American Tobacco Co.* v. *U. S.*, 328 U. S. 781 (1946).

15. *U. S.* v. *United Shoe Machinery Corp.*, 110 F. Supp. 295 (1953).

16. Judge Wyzanski ordered that these practices be abandoned and that patents be licensed to competitors. When the company's share of the total market was still 60 percent a decade later, the government insisted on further remedy and by Supreme Court decision in 1969 the company was forced to reduce its share of the market to one-third.

17. *Appalachian Coals, Inc.* v. *U. S.*, 288 U. S. 344 (1933).

18. *City of Philadelphia* v. *Westinghouse Electric Corp.*, 210 F. Supp. 483 (E. D. Penn, 1962).

19. *Eastern States Retail Lumber Dealers Association* v. *U. S.*, 234 U. S. 600 (1914).

20. *Interstate Circuit, Inc.*, v. *U. S.*, 306 U. S. 208 (1939).

21. *American Tobacco* v. *U. S.*, 328 U. S. 781 (1946).

22. See, for example, *Theater Enterprises, Inc.* v. *Paramount Film Distributing Corp.*, 346 U. S. 537 (1954).

23. See, for example, *U. S.* v. *General Motors Corp.*, 384 U. S. 127 (1966).

24. See, for example, *FTC* v. *Eastman Kodak Co.*, 274 U. S. 619 (1927).

25. See *Tampa Electric Co.* v. *Nashville Coal Co.*, 365 U. S. 320 (1961).

26. Despite a decision assuring that Los Angeles discount houses could not be prevented from obtaining automobiles in *U. S.* v. *General Motors Corp.*, 384 U. S. 127 (1966), franchised dealers continue to be the standard pattern in selling automobiles. Dealers must be willing to sell to consumers from each others' areas, however, or they may be found guilty of agreeing to divide markets.

27. *Brown Shoe Co.* v. *U. S.*, 370 U. S. 294 (1962).

28. *U. S.* v. *Philadelphia National Bank*, 374 U. S. 321 (1963).

29. *U. S.* v. *DuPont*, 353 U. S. 586 (1957).

30. See, for example, *FTC* v. *Proctor and Gamble*, 386 U. S. 568 (1967).

31. See, for example, *FTC* v. *Consolidated Foods Corp.*, 380 U. S. 592 (1965).

32. The resulting firm would be required by the SEC to provide sales and income data for any line of business that accounts for 10 percent of sales or more, but in a large corporation many of its activities do not represent 10 percent of its sales, and the sales categories are left to the firms to define so they still have great control in what finally is reported.

Industry 5
After
Antitrust

A trust of the 1890s would combine into one organization many smaller firms in an industry, which the firms through their combination could then control. Such obvious market control cannot survive today because of antitrust effort. Although large business organizations do exist, their form has certainly been influenced by antitrust policy. A large business firm today is more apt to operate in many industries and even many countries than to occupy a dominant position in only one market. Of course vast improvements in transportation and communication and less restrictive trade policies since the turn of the century now put firms from different countries in more direct competition, but antitrust policy has also fostered competition.

Comparisons of market structure before and after our turn-of-the-century antitrust effort are virtually unavailable owing to a lack of comparable data for the different times. Research by Professor Warren Nutter does indicate that 17.4 percent of our national income originated in industries where the top four firms had half or more of sales in the year 1899, whereas in 1958 about 16 percent came from industries with such high concentration [17, p. 82]. A larger change over that period actually occurred in activity classified as governmental or governmentally supervised, rising from 6.5 percent of national income in 1899 to 21.5 percent in 1958.

Having only limited opportunity for comparisons over time, we focus more on the modern day, because more data are available to describe it. We can try to judge in some absolute sense how free the economy is of unwanted antitrust violations like monopolization, and thus the extent to which the policy goals considered in Chapter 2 are being achieved. We shall first examine the modern corporation to see how it has grown and how it is controlled. Next, we turn to individual markets and consider how to represent their structure so we can anticipate its effect on conduct in the market.

Finally, we review findings from studies of firms and industries, using ways to characterize entry difficulty and other distinguishing and important elements of industry structure to see how they are related to industry performance.

THE LARGE CORPORATION TODAY

The market process is far more complex now than in the primarily agrarian economy observed by Adam Smith. Many sophisticated large-scale production processes have been invented or discovered since then and corporations have reached sizes undreamed of in Smith's time. Corporations that have hundreds of thousands of employees and billions of dollars worth of assets located all over the world make formidable adversaries for any national government wanting to oversee their actions.[1] Their factories may be the dominant employers in small communities where a corporate decision to close or relocate operations would be an awful blow. And yet they may not possess the monopoly power in product markets that is opposed by the Sherman Act, or engage in mergers or restraints of trade. Indeed, their power to move resources quickly from one market to another and to enforce good management in their separate divisions may even enhance resource allocation. Still, the possibility that competitive advantages over smaller firms are available to them, together with their sometimes dominant positions in major markets, can raise questions about whether their existence conflicts with antitrust aims.

The accountability of large corporations to the general public, whether for antitrust or for other purposes, is frequently questioned today. Hired managers have to work diligently to maximize profit for the shareholders of a corporation that is subject to demanding competitive pressure in all its product markets, because otherwise neither managers nor firm can survive. But if the corporation possesses monopoly advantage in any of its markets and top managers are not closely controlled by shareholders those managers may indulge their own preferences in the workers they hire [1], in pursuing sales more than profits [4], or in other ways [7, 16, 27]. The managers are seen exercising this power more readily in very large corporations, where no dominant shareholder interest will exist to oppose them [12]. The managers may be able to install officers of the firm on the board of directors, and prevent cumulative voting by shareholders that could allow minority owners to focus their votes and place at least one director on the board. And they have virtually all the resources of the corporation at their disposal in any contest with outsiders over control of the firm. Corporate control is complicated further by the presence of institutional investors such as mutual funds, pension funds, insurance companies, university endowment funds, and other institutional investors, which together hold about half of the stock of companies traded on the New York Stock Exchange. Most of these institutions will not contest a management's action of which they disapprove; they will gradually dispose of their stock holdings instead. While this "voting with the feet" may jolt an incompetent management it is still quite passive and, compared with the oversight of aggressive owners, it probably makes life easier for top executives of large corporations.

In organizing, firms presumably try to balance what is to be done through markets and what is to be handled within the boundaries of the firm itself [4]. In this century firms have grown large by expanding in three main ways. First, they have become more integrated vertically, from raw material to final product, partly through mergers but also through internal growth. Second, they have expanded operations to other countries, and producers from other countries have opened operations here, to create what are called *multinational* firms. And finally, firms have expanded into lines of business quite unrelated to their original purposes until they are described as conglomerate.

Vertical integration can allow economies, of course, as when a steel maker also produces structural shapes and thereby avoids the cost of reheating steel ingots. A steel producer may also explore for iron ore and coal to reduce risks of depending on others for such essential supplies in steel making. Retail grocers may integrate with a wholesale supplier to avoid haggling individually with farmers and processors, and also to reduce risk by gaining assurance of supplies. But apart from such genuine economies there also are potential abuses if one firm is dominant in vertically related markets. In Chapter 4 we saw how the integrated aluminum maker, Alcoa, was accused of making the price of final aluminum products low while keeping the price of aluminum ingots high, thereby squeezing independent fabricators who had to buy ingots and sell final products. Even when competing firms can avoid being exposed to such tactics by integrating fully themselves, more investment will be needed to be in the more integrated line of business. As a result new entry will become more difficult and that can handicap competition. Thus vertical integration can bring economies but it also may open the door for strategic exercise of market power.

Most of our five hundred largest corporations can be called multinational firms because they deal in markets in more than one country. Sometimes vertical integration may take a firm into other countries to obtain raw materials or to reach more consumers. Firms successful in their home countries may also repeat in other countries essentially what they were doing at home, both to capitalize on what they do well and to diversify risks by reducing their dependence on any one country's economy. When a corporation can choose the most advantageous of tax, tariff, license, quota, and other national policies in deciding where to locate its operations, it can limit the power of any one nation to regulate its trade. Since many national trade policies impose losses on the world's citizens by reducing trade, this effect of multinational corporations is not necessarily bad. As multination firms from outside the United States, such as Toyota and Volkswagen to name only two, can demonstrate, they also increase competition. However, by rivaling in power the nation-state that has developed since medieval times, multinational corporations threaten legitimate national authority and some observers find this worrisome.

Since World War II large corporations have diversified into a variety of business activities. The Hershey Company of your childhood is no longer a maker of chocolate candy alone, for example, but sells cookies, bisquits, spaghetti sauce, and electrical appliances, among other things. Such conglomerate firms have the capacity to enter industries that are closed to less powerful firms, so they can make absolute-cost entry barriers less serious. A conglomerate firm can offer a pooling of the risks associated with different products, too, so for those affiliated with it the exposure to total loss is reduced. Of course such pooling is already available to investors who hold large diversified portfolios. But for employees who cannot diversify by holding many jobs at once and for smaller investors who hold only a few securities, conglomerate organization may offer lower risk. Corporate oversight of the product-line divisions of a conglomerate, like the ITT Corporation operating Avis rent-a-car, Continental Baking, or Rayonier Fabrics, is also seen by some observers as an improved means of enforcing efficiency and the goals of owners over managers [25].

The main antitrust objection to multinational or conglomerate firms is similar to that raised against vertically integrated firms, namely that they are able to use income from several markets for strategic purposes in a particular market. A conglomerate or multinational firm can draw on its other activities to wage a price war or other confrontation using its so-called "deep pocket" reserves that may give it advantages over competitors not organized in the same way. The FTC argues that conglomerates can withhold information needed for sound allocation of resources among the many industries, if their reports tell little about industry-by-industry profitability. Multinational firms selling and financing their activities in many countries of the world can make information about their separate activities hard to obtain. Large corporations may also be able to exert influence in Washington, D. C. to obtain beneficial political action.

Whether it was intended that way or not, federal tax policy actually encourages conglomerate organization and growth in corporate size [22]. By pooling a variety of different activities, conglomerate organizations can reduce the risk of bankruptcy, thereby improving the firm's opportunity to borrow capital from banks at interest that is deductible as an expense before taxes rather than use equity capital for which returns are subject to federal income taxation. Also, if a firm grows by reinvesting profit so that equity shareholdings appreciate in value the shareholders can experience what is called a *capital gain* instead of a cash dividend. The rate of tax on capital gain is lower than (usually one-half) the rate of tax on dividend income. So with current taxes a corporation acting in the interests of its shareholders can be expected to diversify; it also will try to grow, and grow, and grow.

MARKET STRUCTURE

It is not easy to classify firms into industries when many firms operate in more than one. The United States Census Bureau has helped by creating the Standard Industrial Classification (SIC) system which provides industry definitions at varying levels of detail (for example, SIC code 20 is food and kindred products; 202 is dairy products; and 2024 is ice cream). It is possible to sort establishments' (plants') outputs into these categories; it also is possible to approximate firms' roles by classifying them in the industries in which they do most of their business.

The main reason we want to identify industries is to analyze them as we would markets. We begin by asking how to characterize their organization in order to predict market conduct or performance. In Chapter 2 we noted a handful of elements thought to reflect the *structure* of an industry in measurable detail more subtle than the extremes of monopoly or competition. These main elements of market structure are: the condition of *entry* to an industry, the industry's *concentration*, the extent of *product differentiation*, the *elasticity of demand*, and *the properties of cost functions* of firms in the industry. Although they may not be ideal, most of these elements can be investigated using real world facts, to be studied for their effects on an industry's conduct and, ultimately, on its performance.

Entry barriers have been measured in several ways. Professor Joe Bain estimated the amount of money needed to establish a firm in an industry at the *minimum efficient scale*, which is a size or scale of operations that would permit operation at an average cost as low as that of established firms in the industry [3]. When very large, that necessary investment can become a barrier to entry, because in imperfect capital markets a new and unknown potential entrant will find it difficult to raise a large sum of money. This capital requirement has been shown empirically to be related negatively to the rate of entry and positively to profit rates [14].

Economies of scale have been estimated also as a percent of the total sales in a market that would be needed to achieve the economies. Recall that a new entrant who must add a significant fraction to industry output in order to reach an efficient scale of operations surely will realize that his entry will cause market price to fall. Anticipating that consequence, the potential entrant may not enter—even when the existing price permits excess profit for already existing firms.

Concentration, as the word suggests, represents how focused and centralized is the decision making in an industry. If there are only a few firms in an industry, and if some of them are much bigger than others, the decisions of the large firm or firms can be controlling. We describe such an industry as concentrated. The simplest and most widely used measure is called the Top-4 concentration ratio, the fraction of industry sales (if other measures such as assets or employees are used instead of sales, the ratio tends to be practically the same) accounted for by the largest four firms. Sometimes the largest eight firms or the largest twenty firms are used (some other countries use the largest three firms). Such measures are usually based on a particular nation's own data, which omit imports; in industries where imports are important, such as automobiles, the measured concentration will therefore be too high. On the other hand, national concentration ratios for products that are costly to ship and have only local markets, like cinder blocks, will understate the actual local market concentration. Aside from such difficulties, a Top-4 concentration ratio of 100 percent would be an example of near monopoly, while something close to zero would reflect ordinary competition. The degree of concentration is expected to affect the way an industry performs, with higher levels of concentration allowing firms to behave more like a monopoly when entry barriers are also present.

Product differentiation is even more difficult to measure. It reflects the extent to which similar products are differentiated in consumers' minds. There may be several toothpastes or cigarettes or beers, but the producer of each attempts to distinguish itself from others and establish in the minds of at least some comsumers a preference for its brand. If the seller is successful it will be more difficult of course for a new entrant to capture sales. The new entrant then will need even more money if he must match high sales promotion expenditures. Because this practice of differentiating products usually calls for extensive advertising it has been crudely represented by advertising expenditures, usually expressed as a percentage of total sales so that firms of different sizes can be compared.

Price elasticity of demand represents the responsiveness of sales quantity to changes in price. It is measured as a ratio of the percentage change in quantity divided by the percentage change in price that prompted the quantity change. Elasticity is included as an element of market structure because it can be important in determining the incentives to collude in an industry. Where demand is highly elastic any increase in price will bring losses in sales for the whole industry and collusion may not be attractive. But where demand is less elastic a small amount of cooperative action by sellers can add much to their profit. For instance, if demand is inelastic an increase in price can actually bring more revenue into the firms. Since quantities will go down, costs could also be reduced, making the profit gain substantial. This influence of elasticity on industry behavior has received only scant empirical attention to date, however, because many problems stand in the way of reliably estimating market demand elasticity.

Cost functions of firms can affect the incentives for alternative pricing actions, much as demand elasticity can. The most important aspect is the extent to which total costs are fixed in the short run or will vary with short-run changes in output. A higher degree of vertical integration might result in more fixed costs in the short run. But a retailer whose main costs are goods to be resold may have a relatively small fraction of fixed costs. If firms are to cooperate by raising price, the immediate gain to them will be greater when there are not many fixed costs in the short run, because they can then save more costs by reducing output as they raise price. If costs are highly fixed there will be almost no immediate saving. Unless the market demand is particularly inelastic, cooperation at a high price will not be so attractive.

MARKET CONDUCT

The structure of a market is expected to influence how the firms in it will behave. Of course suspicions about how market structure might affect market conduct influenced the choice of market structure elements to consider: the condition of entry, the concentration of decision making among rivals, the extent of product differentiation, and the influence on rewards for alternative actions of demand elasticity and cost functions. Any one firm has little scope for influencing market conduct when no barriers limit entry, concentration is low, and products cannot be differentiated. Even at the other extreme, where a monopolist is in control, market conduct is not very interesting because the monopolist can act without challenge to maximize its profit. Market conduct is important to study when entry is difficult and there are a few firms in a market because then their interactions with each other will determine how the industry performs.

Entry barriers protect the firms from intrusion of new rivals when profits are high, while high concentration makes feasible the sort of coordinated, even tacitly cooperative, pricing that will make profits greater than unbridled competition would allow. When entry is difficult and the decisions of a few firms are controlling we have an oligopoly market, in which the firms are able to see the effects their actions have on one another. The fewer the firms and the more protected they are from new entry, the more we might question how vigorously they will compete. We can get an idea how the incentives for each firm to compete or to join in cooperation with

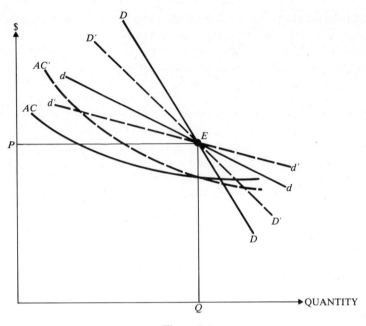

Figure 5.1

others can be influenced by product differentiation, elasticity of market demand, and properties of cost functions by looking at the situation of an individual firm portrayed in Figure 5.1.

The two steep demand curves in Figure 5.1, *DD* and *D'D'*, represent different market demand elasticities, with *D'D'* being the more elastic. For a given market demand elasticity the firm is assumed to have a constant share of market demand as long as all firms have the same price. Thus, if the market price is raised from the current level at point *E*, the individual firm will enjoy more profit when demand is less elastic, the case of demand *DD*. The firm will experience a different response if it changes price unilaterally. Two examples are given to illustrate the response for the firm acting alone, according to the individual firm demand curves *dd* and *d'd'*. The curves are downward sloping on the assumption that each firm produces a product somewhat different from those of other firms and appeals to some consumers. Since a high degree of product differentiation makes products less substitutable in the minds of consumers, the curve *dd* represents a less elastic demand than *d'd'*, and curve *dd* is for the case when products are more highly differentiated. If the firm made a unilateral price increase from point *E* it would be more profitable in that highly differentiated case of demand *dd* than when products are less differentiated along *d'd'*.

Finally, the cost curve AC represents average cost when most costs are variable, so total cost varies greatly with output, whereas AC' represents a case in which more costs are fixed in the short run so total cost does not vary as much with output [24]. The gain from a rise in price and reduction in output will be greater along AC, where total costs vary more with output because fewer costs are fixed. Although Figure 5.1 illustrates roughly the incentives of individual firms in oligopoly markets, those incentives may not dominate. For instance, when a large portion of total cost is fixed the very difficulty of reaching agreement may lead to a history of such violent outcomes that firms will cooperate to avoid repeating them. Historical practices may also help or hinder the firms in reaching cooperative prices. For example, if one major firm has been leading in price changes for years with others willingly following, that could facilitate cooperative orchestration of market price in future.

Some effects of market structure on market conduct can have feedback effects in turn on market structure. Suppose a few firms in an oligopoly market with inelastic demand and a low portion of fixed costs cooperatively reach a price higher than competition would allow. Each may then try to protect its own position by devoting some of its potential profit gain to developing more distinctive product characteristics, that is, by further differentiating its product. The market structure will be affected as a result because product differentiation will become greater. Also, over time in a competitive market firms fail and are replaced, but when entry to an industry is difficult no steady stream of replacements is available and instead the industry will tend to grow more concentrated. Without new entrants to chip away at their positions, a few lucky firms can come to have much of the business. That is one reason high concentration and high entry barriers often occur together, making it difficult to pinpoint the effect on market performance of either element alone.

MARKET PERFORMANCE

Many of the characteristics of modern industry that are called elements of market structure—entry barriers, concentration, product differentiation, cost relationships—have been related in a number of empirical studies to various measures of market performance. The measure most commonly used to represent efficiency has been a firm or industry rate of return on assets, with a persistently high rate of return taken as evidence of more monopolistic performance. Attempts also have been made in empirical studies to evaluate progressiveness, stability, and to a lesser extent fairness or equity. Let us now consider briefly the effects on performance that have been found, looking in turn at efficiency, progressiveness, and stability and equity.

Economic Efficiency

The first effort to examine empirically the relation between industry concentration and the rate of return on assets achieved by leading firms as an indication of industry efficiency was undertaken by Professor Joe S. Bain [2]. He examined forty-two national industries for the period of the late 1930s and found a positive relation between industry rates of return and Top-8-firm concentration ratios. Two major studies of the effects of both concentration and entry barriers on rate of return were carried out by Professor Bain [3] and Professor H. Michael Mann [13], the latter using a sample of thirty industries over the period from 1950 to 1960. These studies relied on estimates of overall entry difficulty that were based on separate estimates of economies of scale, the degree of product differentiation, and other entry barriers such as the capital outlays needed for successful entry. They indicated that entry barriers and concentration each affected profit-rate. Later analysis of their data by Professor Leonard Weiss [25] also showed that concentration had a greater effect on profitability when entry barriers were very high.

Despite the existence of about thirty more studies (many reviewed by Professor Weiss in [25] and [26]), which offer similar findings, the connection between these market structure elements and profit rates is not accepted by all researchers because the observed relations are based on crude data. They do not persist reliably over time and are subject to alternative interpretations [10]. In an effort to avoid these weaknesses other studies have focused on data from firms rather than industries.

Relative firm size, or market share, has been shown in several studies to be an important determinant of a firm's rate of return, more important than industry concentration. Professor Harold Demsetz argued that small firms should enjoy higher profits if the larger firms in the same industry cooperatively avoid price competition. He showed for ninety-five industries in the year 1963 that no such relation between concentration and small-firm profit rates could be found [8]. Instead, the *difference* in profit rates between large firms and small firms was greater within the more concentrated industries.

Absolute firm size has been found positively related to profit rate, too [11]. Large firms may have the advantage noted before of being well known, so they can raise capital more easily in imperfect capital markets and thereby exploit opportunities not open to smaller firms. Economies of scale might continue to be experienced at very large firm sizes also, to account for this greater profitability of larger firms. But a host of cost function studies in many industries indicate that beyond some minimum efficient firm size there are no further economies of scale. Moreover, that minimum efficient size usually is so small that high concentration is seldom necessary to have firms operating at efficient sizes, at least in the United States. To the extent that economies of scale are related to profit rates at the industry level, it is more likely due to their effect as an entry barrier than to any further reduction in average cost the scale economies make possible for already existing firms.

The significant effect that absolute and relative size appear to have on firm rates of return, combined with effects traced to entry barriers and concentration, suggests that some monopolistic advantages may exist in modern industries. Table 5.1 illustrates the market share of the largest firm and the concentration ratio for twelve hard-to-enter U. S. industries, where the circumstances do not appear ideal for fostering competition. But the evidence on actual industry performance is not so unambiguous that monopoly power can be clearly established on a wide scale. We are merely left with the suspicion that some firms hold powerful positions in some markets.

Table 5.1 Market power in industries with high entry barriers

Industry	Market share of largest firm	Market share of top-4 firms (top-4 concentration)
Aircraft and engines	50%	100%
Automobiles	45	85
Cereals	45	95
Computers	70	85
Copying equipment	85	95
Drugs	50*	90*
Heavy electrical equipment	50	100
Iron and steel	35*	70*
Locomotives	75	100
Petroleum refining	35*	70*
Photographic film	70	100
Telephone equipment	95	100

*Adjusted for regional product submarkets.

Source: Clair Wilcox and William G. Shepherd, *Public Policies Toward Business*, 5th ed. (Homewood, Ill.: Richard D. Irwin, Inc., 1975c.), p. 43. Adapted by permission of the publisher.

Progressiveness

To achieve the goal of progressiveness there have been those who argued against a strong antitrust policy on the ground that large, monopolistic firms do the most innovating. Of course this is an empirical proposition. And the weight of evidence does not really support it. Competition may not be an ideal setting for research, since we see little commercial research in industries where Top-4 firm concentration is below 10 percent. But industries with extremely high concentration also do not carry out very much research.

Given the possibility of patent protection, the standard arguments about the effect of market structure on research and innovation go something like this. The competitive firm has a great incentive to innovate and lower its costs, because with a patented invention it could steal the march on its competitors. But with its back pushed to the wall by those very competitors the firm will lack the means to support research. On the other hand, with its profitable position the monopolist has the means to conduct research. The monopolist lacks incentive, though, when its position is already well protected.

The possibility of inventing a new product may be viewed differently from reducing the cost of making an existing product. For both competition and monopoly could enjoy the same gain from an altogether new product and a new market. Of course if the monopolist also had a monopoly in products complementary with the new one, the incentive to develop the new product might be even greater than it would be for the competitive firm in an otherwise similar situation. Conglomerates might even be able to gain more from research, because whenever anything was discovered they would have a better chance of being able to exploit it in one of many operations. Lacking a patent system, or using an imperfect patent system, would work against the competitive firm. The monopolist has market control and therefore can appropriate gains through exploitation of any invention, whereas the competitor will lose the opportunity to appropriate gains as others learn of the invention and duplicate it.

Evidence suggests that, compared with smaller firms, the largest firms in an industry spend the same or a smaller percentage of their sales revenue on research and development.[2] Conceivably economies of scale in conducting research might account for this finding, but other evidence indicates that if anything research and development productivity declines as size of firm increases. There is some evidence that when the cost of innovating is great a monopolist may exploit an invention by innovating sooner than a firm in competition. But diffusion of the results of research and development throughout an industry appears to be slightly faster in less concentrated industries.

Even if the evidence showed that more monopolistic industries were more innovative we still might not want to encourage monopoly as a matter of public policy. For why should research effort occur in those industries where monopoly power exists, rather than in other industries where the research might be more productive? Attacking monopoly while raising a like amount of money to support research through an inefficient tax should allow more progress, if the research can be channeled where it can have a high payoff (for example, in this century in agriculture).

We make no attempt here to assess the degree of progressiveness and compare it with an ideal level. Instead we only consider the effect of market structure on progressiveness. From the evidence no great gain in progressiveness can be expected from relaxing antitrust enforcement. If stronger enforcement reduced the highest levels of concentration it might even stimulate more research.

Stability and Equity

A vigorous campaign against the pricing practices of large corporations was waged in the 1930s by Gardiner Means.[3] The national economy was depressed, and it appeared to him that these large firms in concentrated industries did not lower price, as economic theory would suggest, when demand fell. This question has never been settled satisfactorily, even now. Despite many charges that firms do or do not *administer* prices, or follow *full-cost* or *rigid* pricing, there has been little effort showing why they would wish to do such things. Perhaps changing price can be difficult and costly whereas keeping a stable price might help to keep profit stable, thus improving the value of the firm in the capital market. But keeping prices more stable might cause greater output and employment adjustments, contributing to a less stable economy. Unemployment compensation plans have been shown to introduce undesirable incentives that might affect employment stability in perverse ways, too. Of course stable prices can also benefit consumers, by reducing the need to search for price information. Despite the importance of this question, the role of market power in overall economic stability remains unsettled [20, pp. 308-14].

There has been concern that market power might give rise to discrimination in employment on race, sex, or other grounds. When managers are not entirely controlled by shareholders and by product market competition, and instead have sufficient discretion to follow their own preferences, they may choose as coworkers persons more like themselves [1]. There is some evidence confirming such an effect, either in the greater representation of women and minority groups in more competitive industries or in more comparable wage payments to them there. But some tests have not found such differences so the evidence is not conclusive.

Professors William Comanor and Robert Smiley have calculated the effect of monopoly profit on wealth distribution [6]. They worked out how estimated monopoly profits might be shared by the main income classes, and how the effects could accumulate over time. Taking the degree of monopoly thought to exist in the U. S. economy today, they found that in its absence the distribution of wealth would be more equal than it is. Under assumptions they thought conservative, they estimated that the wealthiest 2.5 percent of our households have 50 percent more wealth now than they would experience if all monopoly were eliminated.

Since monopoly and its advantages go against the grain of our society's main principles, most citizens probably would agree (especially if they owned no part of any monopoly firm) that without monopoly, the income distribution would be fairer. Antimonopoly effort thus would seem appropriate from an equity as well as an efficiency standpoint. But there is the problem, alluded to earlier, that current holders of some monopoly positions bought them (perhaps from original monopolists) at a capital value that allows them only a competitive return. Perhaps the monopoly still should be eliminated; then buyers of shares would be more careful to avoid paying large sums for monopoly positions in future. But there is a question of fairness there that needs to be faced.

SUMMARY

Does an industry that is not concentrated and is easy to enter perform better than one that is difficult to enter and that has much of its sales concentrated in the hands of just a few firms? Although open to criticism, there is evidence that will support the answer of "yes." Larger firms in more concentrated industries with high entry barriers earn greater returns on equity, indicating that they may exercise market power in setting prices. And there is no persuasive evidence that those who possess market power redeem themselves by carrying out more research and development activity. Of course an ideal level of progressiveness may be impossible to define, but no great harm to the rate of technological change need follow the dissolution of large firms or the elimination of market power. If any effect of monopoly on stability and full employment can be discerned, it probably goes in the direction of reducing the stability of working hours, although this remains largely an open question. The claim has been made that monopoly profit has tended to make less equal and fair the distribution of wealth in society.

Based on turn-of-the-century tendencies we observed in Chapter 3, the enforcement accomplishments of Chapter 4 seem to have had some effect in reducing the degree of monopoly, and that should help in achieving all the goals we noted.[4] Remaining monopolistic elements indicate a lack of complete success for antitrust policy, however. So, unless they would prove prohibitively expensive, new antitrust laws or better enforcement of existing laws seem to deserve attention.

REFERENCES

1. Armen A. Alchian and Reuben A Kessel. "Competition, Monopoly, and the Pursuit of Pecuniary Gain." In *Aspects of Labor Economics*. Princeton, N. J.: Princeton University Press, 1962.

2. Joe S. Bain. "Relation of Profit Rate to Industry Concentration: American Manufacturing: 1936-40." *Quarterly Journal of Economics* 65: 293-324 (August 1951).

3. Joe S. Bain. *Barriers to New Competition*. Cambridge, Mass.: Harvard University Press, 1956.

4. William J. Baumol. *Business Behavior, Value and Growth*. rev. ed. New York: Harcourt Brace Jovanovich, 1967.

5. Ronald Coase. "The Nature of the Firm." *Economica* 4: 386-405 (November 1937).

6. William S. Comanor and Robert H. Smiley. "Monopoly and the Distribution of Wealth." *Quarterly Journal of Economics* 89: 177-94 (May 1975).

7. Richard M. Cyert and James G. March. *A Behavioral Theory of the Firm*. Englewood Cliffs, N. J.: Prentice-Hall, 1963.

8. Harold Demsetz. "Industry Structure, Market Rivalry, and Public Policy." *Journal of Law and Economics* 15: 1-9 (April 1973).

9. Joel B. Dirlam and Alfred E. Kahn. *Fair Competition*. Ithaca, N. Y.: Cornell University Press, 1954.

10. Harvey J. Goldschmid, H. Michael Mann, and J. Fred Weston, eds. *Industrial Concentration: The New Learning*. Boston, Mass.: Little, Brown, 1974.

11. Marshall Hall and Leonhard Weiss. "Firm Size and Profitability." *Review of Economics and Statistics* 49: 319-31 (August 1967).

12. William A. McEachern. *Managerial Control and Performance*. Lexington, Mass.: D. C. Heath, 1975.

13. H. Michael Mann. "Seller Concentration, Barriers to Entry, and Rates of Return in Thirty Industries, 1950-1960." *Review of Economics and Statistics*. 48: 295-307 (August 1966).

14. Edwin Mansfield. "Entry, Gibrat's Law, Innovation and the Growth of Firms." *American Economic Review* 52: 1023-51 (December 1962).

15. Edwin Mansfield. *Industrial Research and Technological Innovation*. New York: W. W. Norton and Co., 1968.

16. Robin Marris. *The Economic Theory of Managerial Capitalism*. Glencoe, Ill.: The Free Press of Glencoe, 1964.

17. G. Warren Nutter and Henry A. Einhorn. *Enterprise Monopoly in the United States: 1899-1958*. New York: Columbia University Press, 1969.

18. Richard A. Posner. *Antitrust Law: An Economic Perspective*. Chicago: University of Chicago Press, 1976.

19. S. J. Prais. *The Evolution of Giant Firms in Britain*. Cambridge: Cambridge University Press, 1976.

20. F. Michael Scherer. *Industrial Market Structure and Economic Performance*. Chicago: Rand McNally, 1970.

21. F. Michael Scherer, Alan Beckenstein, Eric Kaufer, and R. Dennis Murphy. *The Economics of Multi-Plant Operation*. Cambridge, Mass.: Harvard University Press, 1975.

22. Roger Sherman. "How Tax Policy Induces Conglomerate Mergers." *National Tax Journal* 25: 521-30 (December 1972).

23. Roger Sherman. *The Economics of Industry*. Boston, Mass.: Little, Brown, 1974.

24. Roger Sherman. *Oligopoly: An Empirical Approach*. Lexington, Mass.: D. C. Heath, 1972.

25. Leonard W. Weiss. "Quantitative Studies of Industrial Organization." In *Frontiers of Quantitative Economics*, edited by Michael D. Intriligator. Amsterdam: North-Holland, 1971.

26. Leonard W. Weiss. "The Concentration-Profits Relationship and Antitrust." In [9].

27. Oliver E. Williamson. *The Economics of Discretionary Behavior*. Englewood Cliffs, N. J.: Prentice-Hall, 1964.

28. Oliver E. Williamson. *Corporate Control and Business Behavior*. Englewood Cliffs, N. J.: Prentice-Hall, 1970.

END NOTES

1. Two excellent studies recently examined the economies available to large firms [21] and reasons for their growth [19].

2. A vast amount of evidence has accumulated on these issues. For a brief summary see [15].

3. For a review of this pricing controversy see [20] or [23].

4. Reconciling goals can be a difficult task itself. On this subject see [9, pp. 18-23] and [18, pp. 18-22].

Reforms 6

Once a young upstart country, the United States now leads the world in the production of most finished goods; its economic power is immense. The degree of concentration of this power within the economy has almost certainly been affected by antitrust laws, although exact effects have not been easy to trace. And in important areas the antitrust laws remain ambiguous as guides to business firm behavior, while their mixture of legislation and case law makes them difficult to administer. Thus it is not surprising that new proposals for reforming antitrust law have been made from time to time. Here we shall examine some of the alternative approaches that have been suggested.

The history of antitrust cases under present law reveals no very clear policy aim [14]. Attempts to relate antitrust effort to the degree of market concentration, or to social benefits that might be obtained, have not succeeded either, although antitrust activity seems to be related to industry sales [1, 9, 17]. The FTC has even stood in the way of better market performance at times, as when it prevented the advertising of tar and nicotine content in cigarettes [13, p. 69]. Even in areas where policy makers feel they can have effects, such as mergers, the ultimate outcome is disappointing [4]. Court cases take years to settle and the remedies they impose take years ✓ longer, if they are ever of significant effect.

Based on studies of effects of market structure on performance reported in Chapter 5 it can be argued that some monopoly power remains in the economy today. Larger firms in more concentrated industries where entry is difficult earn above-average rates of return. The largest firms in concentrated industries also may devote less attention to research. And the concentrated industries may offer less stable work opportunity. The monopoly power we still have may also make incomes less equal. These findings lead one to ask whether the current law could be better enforced or perhaps reformed. Even for one who questions these findings and believes antitrust policy already is effective in restraining monopoly there are reforms to consider, for antitrust policy is costly and some of its features can be criticized as not the best ways to achieve the effects.

Reform proposals are of three main types. First, there are proposals that would keep existing law but change its administration by changing procedures, revising the penalties imposed for violations, closing loopholes, and pursuing difficult cases more aggressively. Second, there are so-called structural proposals that would operate in some way on the market structure of industries to ensure that competition has scope to function. And, third, there are proposals aimed at controlling the corporation by requiring, at least of large firms, federal incorporation that could be fashioned to achieve a variety of aims. These three types of proposals will be discussed in turn.

MAKING PRESENT LAW MORE EFFECTIVE

We shall sketch four areas where proposals would make present law more effective: improved legal procedures, revised penalties for antitrust violation, the elimination of antitrust immunities, and more aggressive enforcement of difficult oligopoly market problems involving tacit collusion.

Legal Procedures

A host of legal procedures can affect antitrust law and its enforcement. Legal procedures influence who has standing to sue, what investigative powers can be used by the FTC or the Justice Department, whether an action can be denied while its legality is being questioned or only after it is found unlawful, and so on. In part because delays can be so important in preventing antitrust justice, procedures that speed court cases without infringing rights are certainly to be welcomed. There are so many possible procedural changes in these complex legal proceedings, however, that we cannot consider many here.

A good example of procedural change is the Antitrust Improvements Act of 1976. As noted in Chapter 3, that act allowed state attorneys general to sue on behalf of their constituents. Legal procedures built up in federal rules of procedure and in previous court decisions had handicapped such actions before the 1976 law. For example, formal notice might have to be given to all parties involved in such a case when the loss experienced by each person was very small and even identifying them by name would be costly. The act also broadened the U. S. attorney general's power to investigate possible antitrust offenses. Before the act the U. S. attorney general could only demand documentary evidence held by parties under investigation but now any person who possesses relevant information, not just as documents alone, can be required to yield it. Finally, the act requires that before a merger involving more than $100,000,000 worth of assets can be completed, the Justice Department and the FTC are to be notified and given thirty days in which to indicate whether they will seek an injunction to oppose the merger. All of these are essentially procedural matters that give advantages to those who enforce antitrust laws.

Penalties

After making a careful study of antitrust penalties Professors Kenneth G. Elzinga and William Breit concluded that no penalty is as effective as a fine, even though it has been used only sparingly [5]. They point out that incarceration can be considered similar to a fine, for some level of fine will probably be judged as an equivalent penalty by an individual facing a particular jail sentence. Since incarceration keeps the guilty person from his most productive work, however, it is inefficient compared with the fine, and therefore inferior. A fine also can avoid perverse treble-damage suits because it gives no prize and thus does not motivate nuisance actions. Of course it also lacks the enforcement incentive of the treble-damage provision, but Elzinga and Breit argue that a more systematic attack is preferred anyway to this bounty-hunter approach to enforcement.

Professor Richard Posner also urges a more rational use of fines in antitrust enforcement [15]. He argues the current unpredictability of fines limits their deterrent value. Rather than merely specifying an upper limit for fines he suggests the general rule that for each offense of the same seriousness, the product of the fine times the probability of detection be made approximately equal. Then a potential offender could expect the same loss on average for undertaking each of the comparable offenses. Since the probability of detecting an antitrust violation is usually quite low, a fine would have to be large if it is to deter antitrust violation. But this very point is seen as an advantage by Professors Elzinga and Breit [5] because the resulting gamble about being caught would be unattractive to a risk-averse businessman. It may seem inequitable to have only a small portion of offenders punished while many escape, but if a deterrent effect can be achieved with a low probability of detection and large fines, only modest enforcement efforts would be needed. And the fines also would go to government as a source of revenue to help pay the costs of enforcement.

A penalty somewhat like a fine is a *tax*, which was discussed as a possible remedy when the Sherman Act was first being debated. Professor Geoffry Shepherd recently has pointed out a variety of ways that a tax might be used as a treatment for current antitrust problems [16]. One proposal would be to place a tax on market share; as a firm came to dominate its market it would have to pay a larger tax. Of course, to be workable the tax would require very clear industry definitions. Such a treatment could also be called structural, since it is aimed at market structure rather than firm behavior. Firm behavior as well as market structure might be modified by taxation, however. For example, if advertising is judged a wasteful expenditure because firms merely offset one anothers' efforts, it might be taxed, or at least no longer counted as a tax-deductible expense. Firm behavior would change because advertising would become relatively more costly. Another tax reform would be elimination of the different effective taxation rates for interest payments, dividends, and capital gains. Present taxation encourages growth in order to take advantage of lower tax rates on capital gain than income. Also, it favors conglomerate organization that allows more use of debt with its tax-deductible interest costs.

Antitrust Immunities

Congress and the courts have allowed important exemptions from antitrust law. We noted briefly in Chapter 3 the main areas that are in some way exempt; in addition to labor they include banking, insurance, transportation, exporting, agriculture, public utilities, fishing, and baseball. Limited protection has also been granted from time to time in newspapers, sports broadcasting, and the learned professions. Some immunity from antitrust prosecution may be justifiable in certain circumstances, as in the 1930s when agricultural produce marketing agreements and some transportation arrangements were allowed in the hope they would help the economy. Such circumstances seldom last for long, however; removing obsolete immunities would be one way of improving antitrust enforcement.[1]

Recently there has been a gradual trend toward broader application of antitrust law: in labor activities when they directly affect final product price, in public utility activities not mandated by explicit state action, in railroad and air cargo transportation, in the practice of law, and in other areas. Rate-setting agreements under state insurance regulation are claimed to allow more effective collusion than is deemed necessary yet they are exempt from antitrust law by act of Congress.[2] The right of farmers to combine collectively for processing, handling, and marketing their products[3] without being accused of restraint of trade is also criticized, especially in milk marketing where legislation[4] authorizes the secretary of agriculture to control prices in a manner intended to boost farmers' incomes. And the right of shipping companies to join in rate-setting conferences,[5] overseen only loosely by the Federal Maritime Commission, has been opposed because it can seriously limit competition.

Many of these immunities from antitrust enforcement show how special interest groups can have the law work to their advantage. Removing them clearly would improve the competitiveness and the efficiency of the economy.

Oligopoly

Many researchers think that existing antitrust law fails to reach tacit collusion in oligopolistic markets. Their conclusion can be supported by observation of enforcement efforts in oligopolistic markets since the early 1950s, where the primary antitrust effort to prevent a worsening of the oligopoly situation has been against mergers. But many industries already are oligopolistic and explicit collusion may not be necessary in such industries before a few relatively large firms can enjoy higher profit rates if new entry is difficult. A resistance to expansion arises naturally in such firms, once they become large enough in their markets to see that expansion will force lower prices and thus reduce profit rates. That relative size may affect *independently* the incentives of firms in this way goes to the heart of the debate over antitrust policy.

Professor Richard Posner has argued that apart from outright monopoly, ensuring independent rather than collusive behavior by firms is an adequate goal of antitrust policy. He argues further than current law can reach that goal [15]. Aggressive enforcement would be required, based on careful analysis of markets with structures that would encourage collusion. In such circumstances, the appearance of price discrimination, constant market shares, exchange of price information, and a number of other practices would be counted by Posner as evidence of collusion. There is some doubt whether this standard for collusive behavior is defined well enough in an oligopoly market to capture mutually beneficial actions by firms, however. Recent evidence indicates that independent behavior by relatively large firms in industries that are difficult to enter might itself lead to higher-than-competitive prices, so independent behavior itself may be inadequate as a goal. If Posner's stronger enforcement will not work then controlling oligopoly may call for new law. Such new law would tend to be of the structural sort.

CONTROLLING MARKET STRUCTURE

In March 1973, the late Senator Philip A. Hart introduced in Congress a proposed Industrial Reorganization Act that defined monopoly to exist: (1) when any firm consistently enjoyed more than a specified profit rate, (2) when there was an absence of price competition in an industry, or (3) when the top-four-firm concentration in an industry persistently was above 50 percent. As the primary remedy for such monopoly, the law would offer deconcentration via divestiture. This new proposal thus would define and attack *de facto market power*, rather than a firm's *intent* or *behavior*, which can be deemed monopolistic under existing antitrust law. It includes provisions recommended as early as 1934 by University of Chicago economist

Henry Simons [18] and since then by authors Carl Kaysen and Donald F. Turner [8] (the latter was chief of the Antitrust Division of the Justice Department from 1965 to 1968), by a task force report on antitrust policy for President Johnson [12], and by consumer advocate Ralph Nader.[6]

To be specific, the proposed Industrial Reorganization Act would define monopoly this way:

There shall be a rebuttable presumption that monopoly power is possessed

(1) by any corporation if the average rate of return on net worth after taxes is in excess of 15 per centum over a period of five consecutive years out of the most recent seven years preceding the filing of a complaint, or

(2) if there has been no substantial price competition among two or more corporations in any line of commerce in any section of the country for a period of three consecutive years out of the most recent five years preceding the filing of a complaint, or

(3) if any four or fewer corporations account for 50 per centum (or more) of sales in any line of commerce in any section of the country in any year out of the most recent three years preceding the filing of the complaint.

The first two of these criteria seem to offer little promise as guides for identifying monopoly. A rate of return persistently above 15 percent can easily be avoided by any firm; all the firm has to do is be wasteful. For years a lack of price competition has been impossible to identify convincingly so it is not apt to be recognized now merely because it is defined as evidence of monopoly power. But the third criterion, which limits the fraction of a market that can be held by a leading firm, is neither as escapable as the first nor as ambiguous as the second.

The proposal by Senator Hart for an upper limit on industry concentration, which to be effective would take the form of a limit on the market share of any one firm, is called a *structural* proposal because it operates on the structure of an industry and not the intent or the behavior of the firms in it. A structural rule would be simpler to enforce than present antitrust law. Whether it is desirable depends, however, on how reliably market structure affects market performance. For only if a particular structure is not inevitable and also has undesirable effects on performance would control over market structure seem worthy of consideration. The soundness for policy of the Hart proposal depends in particular on how a firm's market share affects its performance, because using concentration as the monopoly criterion would focus, at least implicitly, on the market shares of leading firms.

An upper limit on market share could help to remedy at one stroke two current problems with the structure of industrial markets: (1) the existence of barriers to new entry, which are virtually impossible to eliminate directly, and (2) the presence in some industries of a few large, dominant firms. We know that new entry into an industry can be difficult for genuine technological reasons, as when a firm must operate at a large scale or a significant fraction of its market in order to achieve reasonably low average cost. When new entry is difficult there will be a tendency over time for some existing firms to have large shares of their industry's sales. This outcome may be due to the absence of fresh new challengers, however, rather than to any greater service the surviving firms perform. Yet technology will yield no feasible way to make new entry into such industries easier or to prevent the greater concentration that will almost inevitably result without it.

Firms with large market shares tend empirically to enjoy higher profit rates. It is unlikely that this greater profitability of larger firms is due to economies of scale, since in those same industries firms experience constant rather than decreasing average cost as their sizes are greater [7]. More reasonably, it can be attributed to the stronger market positions enjoyed by the relatively larger firms. To be sure, economists do not agree completely about how the economic performance of an industry will be affected by all the market structure elements—elements such as economies of scale, the amount of capital required for new entry into an industry at an efficient size, the extent of product differentiation, and concentration—but the weight of evidence we considered in Chapter 5 suggests large firms in industries that are difficult to enter may enjoy market power.

An upper limit on market share could prevent the erosion of competition that may follow naturally when a few firms come to dominate an industry that is difficult to enter. Rather than rely on an uncertain and costly process of litigation to break up dominant firms, as we might do in extreme cases under present law, a market-share limit could harness the self-interest of the firms themselves to choose the best way to divide into effective organizations, and the most appropriate time for it as well. To comply with such a law, the owners could choose, or managers could choose in their owners' interests, when and how to split themselves. Corporations then would not go on to grow large and powerful in their industries, a result that otherwise tends to be brought about simply by the lack of new entrants.

Of course while operating under a market-share limit it is possible that managers will not serve owners faithfully. Managers may prefer to maintain a large size, perhaps by operating just under the market-share limit, even though a more radical division of the firm would benefit shareholders more in the long run. That is a problem of control over the corporation for which other reforms have been proposed.

CONTROLLING CORPORATIONS

The early twentieth century economist and social critic Henry Simons blamed many antitrust problems on failure to control effectively the chartering of corporations. He sympathized with classical English liberals, for whom powerful government was inimical to individual liberty, but he saw as a corollary to their arguments the need for explicit limits to private economic power as well. And of the government's attention to this duty he said "[w]e may recognize, in the almost unlimited grants of powers to corporate bodies, one of the greatest sins of governments against the free enterprise system" [18, p. 52]. He strongly criticized the loss of real control over corporate chartering by the separate states after 1890. Even though chartered in only one state, a corporation had constitutional guarantees that allowed it to operate nationally. So a corporation could pit one state against another to obtain the terms it wanted; that led to what Simons saw as the "careless, extravagant dispensing of corporate powers."

The absolute size of a corporation might be limited most easily through incorporation laws. Simons, who also was an early proponent of structural market-share limits, urged absolute limits on firm size in 1934 [18]. More recently, two studies of antitrust policy recommended some sort of absolute limit to firm size. The Ralph Nader study group [6] would limit a corporation's assets to $2 billion, except for regulated monopolies. Although it made no proposals to limit absolute firm size, President Johnson's White House Task Force Report on Antitrust Policy urged that no mergers be allowed between firms if one had annual sales of $500 million or assets of $250 million [12]. The idea behind a statutory limit on firm size would be to control how large a corporation could grow, much as earlier state incorporation laws had done by limiting the total value of assets it could hold. Such an absolute limitation would affect industry concentration or market shares only in the industries where firms are large, industries such as oil, steel, and automobiles. An absolute size limit would amount implicitly to a relative size limit in such industries.

An absolute size limit is not concerned so directly with the process of product market competition, however. It would limit the growth of conglomerate firms, even if they had only a small relative share in each of many markets. The absolute size limit is intended to prevent any large concentration of economic power that might influence political institutions inordinately, or be excessively powerful relative to workers, suppliers of capital, or suppliers of other inputs, as well as consumers. Any effort to limit firm size remains in part a political effort. Concern about forms of absolute power go back to the eighteenth century in England when classical English liberalism took its position against concentrated *government* power on the ground that it would threaten political liberty. History shows that this position did not ensure economic liberty, for without any limits to restrain them employers grew powerful enough to exploit workers and perpetrate a variety of injustices which were later criticized so eloquently by Karl Marx and others. The reaction to this economic power in England, and in a different way in the United States as well, was to enlarge government, whereas direct limits to the economic power might have been preferable.

As in the case of market-share limits, a statutory limit on firm size could harness the judgments of firms' managers, rather than the opinions of district court judges, in deciding how and when to divide a growing firm. Absolutely sharp limits might be moderated by imposing a gradually rising tax as any size limit is further exceeded, similar to that proposed by Shepherd for market shares [16]. Genuine problems arise, though, in deciding how large the limit should be and how it should be expressed, and these problems are aggravated by the need to keep the limit current despite changes in the price level and in technology. Whether the limit is in assets or number of employees might depend, for example, on the harm that was thought to follow from control over either resource; even though limits might be set for both measures it would be difficult to justify any very exact level. Of course genuine scale economies may be forgone (and perhaps not even discovered!) if a size limit is set below the range where they could be realized.

Many other purposes also could be served by federal control of incorporation. For one thing, federal incorporation requirements would probably be enforced, whereas for the same reasons they are lenient in their incorporation requirements states now make only token enforcement efforts. A corporation is supposed to pursue the purpose approved in its charter, for example, but most states neither insist on a definitive statement of purpose nor compare actual practice with the avowed purpose. Besides enforcing incorporation provisions, unified federal incorporation might help to enforce other laws as, for instance, the present Clayton Act prohibitions against interlocking directorates. Or for another example, Securities and Exchange Commission registration and publicity requirements to protect investors easily could be included as duties set out in a corporation's charter.

Genuine control of incorporation actually could create a wide range of instrumentalities for limiting firm organization and industry behavior. For instance, consider placing a limit on the number of shares of stock a firm could issue, as a gradual restraint on firm size. Once a firm had reached the limit its continued growth would lead to higher and higher share values until some inconvenience in trading them would result. Many investors could not hold a share worth, say, $20,000. Although mutual funds might not mind dealing in such valuable shares, a loss of share marketability among smaller investors would have to be expected. The main point here is not whether this particular way to limit firm size is good or bad, but rather that with control over incorporation many subtle instruments would become available for controlling corporations.

Control of incorporation at the federal level is not without drawbacks, however. After all, monopoly control over any activity may be abused, and a federal monopoly for corporate chartering is no exception. One or more of many state government agencies may find new procedures or ideas that would not have been discovered in the single agency alone. When corporations have a choice of state offices they may also receive better service. Reaching agreement on uniform provisions could be much more difficult at the federal level, and frequent changes in the form for corporate organization, which might accompany disagreements, would not be desirable either. Federal incorporation need not alter current arrangements at the state level, however, particularly if, as the Ralph Nader proposal recommends [11], federal incorporation were to be required only of large firms with sales over $250 million or more than 10,00 employees.

Since the private corporation receives valuable privileges from society it is not unreasonable to insist that safeguards against abuse of such privileges be strong. Despite the discussion among professional managers of their "social responsibility," they have had only limited accountability to society [10] for many years. Early incorporation laws pressed accountability on officers of corporations [3] and were somewhat effective because firms were small and officers could be held responsible for their actions. But lenient incorporation laws and the growth of corporations to gigantic sizes made public responsibilities of officers difficult to enforce. Recent efforts to enforce obligations of directors and top managers of corporations have come from government regulators concerned with health and occupational safety, environment, equal employment opportunity, product safety, or other matters, and also from shareholders who question director or management actions. But these efforts seem to have fostered uncertainty rather than clear rules of liability, and corporations have responded by purchasing liability coverage to protect officers and directors, so any aim of enforcing personal responsibility has been somewhat deflected. Compared with these efforts, clearer incorporation laws might bring more exact definition of accountability for officers and directors of corporations.

SUMMARY

We opened this book by referring to Art Nouveau, a late nineteenth century development in the arts that led to modern design. From that same time came our present antitrust law, parts of which remain vague and unclear in the present day. The most extreme turn-of-the-century abuses have been stopped by these antitrust laws and their enforcement. The resulting antitrust policy remains an impressive achievement that has no doubt contributed to our nation's economic well-being. But laws designed for another age leave many important issues unsettled today. The laws are not in a form that is clear and easy to administer or ideally suited to modern technologies. So a time for improvement of antitrust law seems at hand.

The suggestions for antitrust policy that were posed in this chapter are intended to stimulate your thinking about alternative arrangements. For, while antitrust law has no doubt altered U. S. industry and reduced extreme monopoly control, the overall record nevertheless shows inconsistency and often ineffectiveness in achieving avowed aims. The aims have not been free of ambiguity either. Relying for policy on court interpretation of vague statutes simply has inherent limitations, partly because those subject to the policy have recourse to courts to resist it and the courts lack clear legislative guidance as to how the issues should be settled. Of course the problem of control over industry structure involves political as well as technical economic questions. But as the economic questions are settled we should expect better laws to put the results into effect.

REFERENCES

1. Peter Asch. "The Determinants and Effects of Antitrust Activities." *Journal of Law and Economics* 13: 575-81 (October 1975).

2. Edward F. Cox, Robert C. Fellmeth, and John E. Schulz. *The Nader Report on the Federal Trade Commission*. New York: Grove Press, 1969.

3. Joseph S. Davis. *Essays in the Early History of American Corporations*. Cambridge, Mass.: Harvard University Press, 1917.

4. Kenneth G. Elzinga. "The Antimerger Law: Pyrrhic Victories." *Journal of Law and Economics* 12: 43-78 (April 1969).

5. Kenneth G. Elzinga and William Breit. *The Antitrust Penalties*. New Haven, Conn.: Yale University Press, 1976.

6. Mark J. Green, Beverly C. Moore, Jr., and Bruce Wasserstein. *The Closed Enterprise System*. New York: Bantam Books, 1972.

7. J. Johnston. *Statistical Cost Analysis*. New York: McGraw-Hill, 1960.

8. Carl Kaysen and Donald F. Turner. *Antitrust Policy: An Economic and Legal Analysis*. Cambridge, Mass.: Harvard University Press, 1959.

9. William F. Long, Richard Schramm, and Robert Tollison. "The Economic Determinants of Antitrust Activity." *Journal of Law and Economics* 16: 351-64 (October 1973).

10. Arthur Selwyn Miller. *The Modern Corporate State*. Westport, Conn.: Greenwood Press, 1976.

11. Ralph Nader, Mark Green, and Joel Seligman. *Taming the Giant Corporation*. New York: W. W. Norton, 1976.

12. Phil C. Neal, Chairman. "The White House Task Force Report on Antitrust Policy." Washington, D. C.: Bureau of National Affairs, 1969.

13. Richard A. Posner. "The Federal Trade Commission." *University of Chicago Law Review* 37: 47-89 (Autumn 1969).

14. Richard A. Posner. "A Statistical Study of Antitrust Enforcement." *Journal of Law and Economics* 13: 365-419 (October 1970).

15. Richard A. Posner. *Antitrust Law: An Economic Perspective*. Chicago: University of Chicago Press, 1976.

16. William G. Shepherd. *The Treatment of Market Power.* New York: Columbia University Press, 1975.

17. John J. Siegfried. "The Determinants of Antitrust Activity." *Journal of Law and Economics* 13: 559-74 (October 1975).

18. Henry Simons. *Economic Policy for a Free Society.* Chicago: University of Chicago Press, 1948.

END NOTES

1. See the Justice Department's "Report of the Task Group on Antitrust Immunities," Washington, D. C.: U. S. Government Printing Office, 1977.

2. McCarron-Ferguson Act, 15 U. S. C. Sec. 1011 et seq. (1970).

3. Capper-Volstead Act, 7 U. S. C. Secs. 291, 292 (1970).

4. Agricultural Adjustments Act, 7 U. S. C. Sec. 601 et seq. (1970).

5. Shipping Act of 1916, as amended in 1961, 46 U. S. C. Sec. 801 et seq. (1970).

6. See the Nader Study Group reports [2] and [6]. The limit on concentration is proposed in [6].

Index